BETW_____

MONSTERS

& Mercy

AN INSPIRING TRUE STORY OF A SOUL LOST & FOUND

BETWEEN MONSTERS

Mercy

AN INSPIRING TRUE STORY OF A SOUL LOST & FOUND

KELLY THOMPSON

CFI
An imprint of Cedar Fort, Inc.
Springville, Utah

This is not an official publication of The Church of Jesus Christ of Latter-day Saints. The opinions
and views expressed herein belong solely to the author and do not necessarily represent the opinions
or views of Cedar Fort, Inc. Permission for the use of sources, graphics, and photos is also solely the
responsibility of the author.

ISBN 13: 978-1-4621-3696-4

Published by CFI, an imprint of Cedar Fort, Inc.
2373 W. 700 S., Springville, UT 84663
Distributed by Cedar Fort, Inc., www.cedarfort.com

   Library of Congress Control Number: 2019956119

Cover design by Shawnda T. Craig
Cover design © 2020 Cedar Fort, Inc.
Edited and typeset by Heather Holm

Printed in the United States of America

10 9 8 7 6 5 4 3 2 1

Dedication

This book is dedicated to every soul whose life has been touched by addiction or mental illness.

"Jesus said unto him, If thou canst believe, all things are possible to him that believeth."

Monsters and Mercy

A place lies between monsters and mercy.
Between the darkest of night and the day.
It's past sadness and sorrow and the fears of tomorrow,
But before joy and hope find their way.

It's not easy to get to,
This mystical sphere,
Where hate leaves a space for the dove.
It's been called illusive,
Barbaric, abusive,
But its design was created in love.

The journey there's tough,
The terrain steep and tall,
This path for the weak and ashamed.
But for the sick and the broken
Carrying burdens unspoken
It's just beyond guilt and the pain.

Do not worry if before you can get there
You collapse and fall to your knees.
For the land that you seek
Is just past "I can do it"
And right before "take this from me."

— Kelly Thompson

Contents

Prologue

"I gotta go, Kelly," Patrick said, without even looking in my direction. There was a long awkward silence, and I realized he meant that it was time for me to get out of the car. This was the first real sentence Patrick had spoken to me since taking my virginity five hours earlier. "But they're not here anymore. They . . . left me," I said, unable to hold back the tears. I wanted to hand Patrick the note I was I holding, but he just stared straight ahead. I glanced into the back seat at our friend, Sean, who sheepishly looked away when I tried to make eye contact with him. "I don't have any way to get home. I live like four hundred miles away. Please, you guys can't just leave me here!" I looked at Patrick and waited for a response. He finally turned his head and looked directly at me. "We gotta go, Kel," he said. This time he said it slowly and more pronounced to be sure I got the message.

Why are they acting like this? I wondered. Sean was my friend, and Patrick—I loved Patrick. I thought he loved me too.

I turned and stared out the window. Panicked thoughts raced through my head: *They're actually going to leave me here.* My heart sank as I accepted the inevitable. I pulled the door handle and slowly stepped out into the hot southern California sun. It was mid-September, but at nearly 90 degrees, it felt a lot more like mid-July. I closed the door and watched as they sped away. *He didn't even say goodbye*, I thought. I looked at the note in my hand and re-read it.

> Kelly,
>
> You weren't here when it was time to check out so we left. You will need to find your own way home. You can call us at your Dad's apartment. We will be there cleaning it out.
>
> 714-555-3838
>
> Mom

Wiping the tears from my eyes, I walked toward the hotel. I opened the lobby door and the cool air washed over me, sending a shiver through my body. "May I use your phone please?" I asked the woman at the front desk. "Sure," she said. When she handed me the receiver, I noticed her name tag said "Brenda." I dialed the number in the note.

The phone rang, and on the other end, my sister Kari answered, "Hello?"

"Is Mom there?" I asked.

While I waited for my mom to pick up, I noticed Brenda watching me intently. She looked confused. When my mom checked out and left the note hours earlier with explicit instructions to give it to me when I showed, she had expected an adult to walk through the door. Seeing a fifteen-year-old walk in and ask where her family went must have caught her off guard. She looked as though she wasn't sure what to think. I turned my head attempting to get some privacy.

"But, Mom. I tried to get here in time . . ."

"Mom, I'm sorry . . ."

"I'm sorry! . . ."

"I know you waited all night . . ."

I could feel Brenda watching as I completely lost control and began sobbing into the phone, begging not to be left without a way home.

"Please don't leave me here . . ."

"I don't have any money . . ."

"Mom, I don't even know how to get home from here! . . ."

"I'm sorry . . ."

"Okay . . . okay . . . bye."

I handed the phone back to Brenda. "Thank you," I said as I sniffled and wiped my runny nose with the inside of my shirt. She stood there looking at me and I felt completely transparent. Suddenly, I became aware that I was still wearing the same clothes I had worn to my father's burial yesterday and I felt an overwhelming urge to take a shower.

Pushing the glass doors open, I walked out into the heat and sat on the curb in some shade to await my rescue—or wait to die. I didn't know which. Thoughts began to race through my mind, and I tried to grasp the entirety of the last few days.

"My dad is dead," I said. "He's dead." As if by repeating it, it would somehow make sense. But it didn't make any sense. "He's dead!" I yelled, but the words fell flat onto the pavement in front of me, and all I could do was sit and stare at them. My forty-six-year-old father had died suddenly from a heart attack days earlier, and no matter what I did, my mind still couldn't seem to be reconciled to the reality that he was gone.

"God, I don't understand what's happening. Is this my punishment for everything I've done? Everyone left me," I cried. "Everyone!"

As the loss hit me, a wave of rage washed over me.

"What kind of God are you? What kind of cruel God are you? Where are you, you monster? Where the hell are you?"

Feeling completely abandoned, I put my head in my hands and sobbed. I began to take slow deep breaths to keep my heart from beating right out of my chest. I breathed in through my nose and out through my mouth. I was breathing, but I was also waiting for an answer. I demanded an answer! But there was no response. There was nothing. Just the heat of the day and the sound of cars driving by filled with people who hadn't just lost everyone they loved.

"I mean nothing to you," I cried.

"*I told you*," said The Whisperer.

I glanced down and noticed a roly-poly bug walking slowly by my foot. I reached down, poked it with my finger, and watched curiously as it curled up into a tight little ball.

1.

The Whisperer

In the spring of 1980, our young Mormon family moved to beautiful Minnetonka, Minnesota. Timber Ridge was a cozy middle-class neighborhood nestled on top of a hill in the suburbs of Minneapolis. Green lawns stretched from yard to yard with no dividing fences. Giant oak and maple trees created a lush canopy and stood sturdy and majestic, holding their ground as they had done for a hundred years. Our comfortable three-story home was white with dark brown shutters and sat dead center in the little neighborhood. Surrounded by friendly families with children of all ages, it was the picture perfect place to raise a family. From the moment the six of us drove up in our wood-paneled Jeep Wagoneer pulling a U-Haul trailer, we felt like we were home.

My parents were a charming-looking couple. Mom was tall and beautiful with green eyes that complimented her white porcelain complexion. She had long, thick red hair that she pulled back with barrettes on either side of her head. Always put together, she dressed with an understated sense of class. Dad was good-looking despite some premature balding. He was built sturdy with a little extra around the middle. He had a round face with kind eyes that sparkled when he smiled. Dad had two distinct fashion styles. His career as a consultant in retail marketing and his church callings kept him in suits with crisp white shirts and ties for Sundays and most of the week. But when Saturday rolled around, it was nothing but old T-shirts, worn-out jeans, a cowboy hat, and a pair of hideous black leather loafers that Mom tolerated.

The day we moved in, while unpacking, there was a sturdy knock at the door. My Mom answered it, and a spunky little girl with wavy auburn hair from the house up the lane stood there grinning. "Hi! I'm Molly! You got anyone my age to play with?" Smiling back, and with a wink, my mom said, "I think we might. You look like you're just about Kelly's age." Molly and I were introduced and became instant buddies.

My nickname was "Bright Eyes." I was five years old with big hazel eyes and shoulder-length blonde hair that was usually pulled up into crooked pigtails on either side of my head. Regardless of the weather, I preferred to run around barefoot and often bore scraped knees and elbows from bike riding and climbing trees. Long before the days of distracting technology, we created our own entertainment. In the summertime, I would be found outside palling around with Molly and other friends on our bikes, making forts, and exploring the nearby woods. We went on scavenger hunts, made homemade slip and slides from Hefty bags, and ran through sprinklers until mud squished between our toes. Sometimes my older sisters, Kari and Heather, would coordinate night games like flashlight Capture the Flag with the neighborhood kids. There was something special and exciting on those warm evenings when we were allowed to be out past dark and our normal bedtimes. Slathered head to toe in bug spray, we ran around the neighborhood, playing for hours until the mosquitos (or our parents) forced us inside for bed.

Hot and humid summer days would often bring powerful evening thunderstorms. Many stormy nights, I would sneak into my sister Kari's room and climb into her bed with her. In the pitch black, we would open the window over her bed to let in the wind.

Blankets wrapped around us, we'd watch and listen eagerly as the eerie darkness crept closer and closer, bringing torrential rainfall and often-noisy hail. Whenever a flash of lightning would strike, stretching across and illuminating the sky, we'd slowly count aloud together with excited anticipation . . . "One-one-thousand . . . two-one thousand . . . three-one thousand!" Until finally, we heard an explosive CRASH! of deafening thunder that would roll and shake the house. Squealing and giggling, we'd jump under the covers for safety.

The long bitter Minnesota winters drove us mostly indoors for entertainment. One winter, Mom and Dad moved the furniture out of our dining room to give us more room to play. The large empty room made a perfect gymnastics studio and was long enough for cartwheels and back walkovers. Hour upon hour, my sisters and I choreographed and practiced dances for parental performances. We used our Grease and Annie records that we played on our orange and brown Fisher-Price record player. Our baby brother, Brian, would often be found sitting on the floor, watching his three older sisters play while he sucked his thumb and held tight to his blue blankie.

One morning after a severe winter storm, we woke up to our entire world covered in a thick sheet of ice. Everything the freezing rain touched had turned into shimmering crystal. It was a dazzling wonderland. Trees, bushes, and fences were completely glazed from top to bottom, frozen in time. The weight of the ice had caused some branches to fall, and there were power outages across our area. After getting the confirmation that school was canceled, my sisters and I bundled up and put on our ice skates. With the asphalt covered by a thick sheet of ice, the streets had turned into a virtual skating rink. Thrilled that we didn't have to go to school, we happily joined the other neighborhood kids outside and spent the day skating.

When the Minnesota winter weather was extreme and road conditions were icy, some evenings, Mom would bundle us up in our winter gear and we would happily pile into the Jeep with Dad. Back in those days, before cells phones, sliding off a slick road and getting stranded in below-freezing weather could quickly become a desperate situation. Dad always kept a large tow chain in the back of the Jeep for any roadside emergencies he might come across in his travels.

"Keep your eyes peeled kids!" Dad would say enthusiastically while we scanned the ditches looking for unlucky drivers who had lost control and slid off the road. "Look Dad! There's one!" someone would shout. Pulling carefully to the side of the road, Dad would step out into the blowing snow.

"How you doing tonight? Need some help? I have a chain," he'd say. After grabbing the heavy chain out of the back, we'd all watch with excitement as Dad would get down in the snow and hook it to both vehicles. He'd hop back into the warm car, look at our excited faces, and say, "You ready?"

"Yes!" we'd scream.

Dad would slowly push his foot on the gas and we'd begin to roll forward until suddenly the Jeep jolted and jerked as the chain pulled taut between the two vehicles. We could feel the Jeep slide from side to side using all the engine's power to try and free the other car.

"Go Dad!" we'd yell.

Finally, the Jeep would begin to creep forward dragging the weight of the stranded car behind it. When it was freed, Dad would shake hands with the relieved driver, politely declining any offer of money for the help. "You have a good night now and take care."

"Should we look for another one?"

"Yes!" we'd shout.

During those evenings helping stranded drivers, I was proud and amazed by my dad and his cheerful service. He was my superhero.

As young adults, my parents became converts to The Church of Jesus Christ of Latter-day Saints, and they were married in the Salt Lake Temple in the spring of 1970. My family was like most typical Latter-day Saint families, and religion played a major role in our lives. On Sundays, we'd have church and then come home to spend time together. Mom always cooked a big dinner, and we'd have a family prayer before our meal. We didn't go shopping, out to eat, or go play with our friends on the Sabbath day. It was special day set aside for the Lord, and that was a priority in our home. There were other church supported activities, such as Monday night family home evening, youth programs, church callings, Relief Society night, ward service projects, and more.

Being honest and having integrity were important qualities often talked about in our family discussions. There was a high standard set for doing the right thing. We were raised with many beautiful examples of giving and service. My parents had an open-door policy for struggling teens that needed refuge, missionaries who needed housing, and relatives in need of a room to stay in. We learned that hard work was an admirable trait to possess, and chores were to be done well and on time.

We were taught the reality of Jesus Christ and about the plan of salvation. Knowing those truths came with the responsibility to do our best to live the example that the Lord set and to share the gospel with others. I believed what I was being taught and sensed the truth of it. I remember looking forward to turning eight years old and finally being baptized like my sisters. Our family of seven was complete in the spring of 1982 when our baby sister Hayley arrived.

When I was six and my sister Heather was nine, we lay on her bed and talked about how much we loved the spiritual things we believed. While I can't remember the exact details of the conversation, or even how the discussion began, I do remember that she and I were aware of how bright the room became. I was suddenly filled with a feeling of exceeding joy and love. It felt like the emotion was going to burst out of my little chest. We talked about what we were experiencing, and how much love we had for each other, and for God. Even though we were just little girls, the Spirit was testifying to the truth.

I was a happy child with a future as bright as my nickname. I was carefree and had everything in life to look forward to. Looking at my life and my loving family, no one could have guessed that it was all about to end. We could not have been prepared for the long nightmare that was coming.

When I was seven years old, The Whisperer appeared out of thin air. One day, I noticed my mind was being attacked by a vicious, shaming voice. It wasn't an audible voice, but a constant barrage of negative thoughts. The sadistic presence penetrated and infected my young mind, killing my happy childhood like a deadly virus. Pointing out real and imagined flaws, he seemed to know everything about me. He was always with me, scrutinizing my every thought and action. His cruelty was brutal and nothing was off limits. The Whisperer's message was loud and clear.

"There is something wrong with you . . . You are not lovable."

The effect the intruder had on me was immediate and powerful. Within weeks of being forced to listen to the negativity, I was filled with fear and anxiety. I became self-loathing and developed a strange primal urge to peel myself out of my own skin. I sensed something very bad was happening to me, but I didn't have the insight or words to express it. I was trapped alone with the enemy. The negative thoughts began to wear me down and my mental health began to suffer.

Even at seven years old, the stress of listening to The Whisperer began to affect the relationships in my life. I was almost always on edge and unusually sensitive. I would often overreact to whatever was said to me. Much of the time, people had to walk on eggshells around me or I'd get my feelings hurt and have a complete meltdown. Regular nightmares began waking me up in the night. I can remember laying in my bed in the dark, and the quiet house seemed to make The Whisperer unbearably loud. When the fear and sadness would overwhelm me, I would take my blanket into the hallway where there was a light and try to go back to sleep.

Because the anxiety was often worse around other people, getting me to go to school became a challenge for my parents. I began doing everything I could in a desperate attempt to avoid going. Full-blown panic attacks in the mornings before school became a regular occurrence. At my young age, these panic attacks mimicked temper tantrums, which confused and terrified my parents.

"They don't like you. You don't matter to anyone. You don't matter. You don't matter. You don't matter."

On and on the voice went torturing me relentlessly. Once, while being teased by my sister, I took my fingernails and dug them into my throat. I can remember the shocked look on her face as I screamed at the top of my lungs while dragging my nails through my skin, leaving long bloody marks. That little episode bought me a ride to see my first therapist. After having me draw a picture of my family and asking me a few standard questions, she assured my parents that I was dealing with some normal sibling rivalry. It wasn't long before it became obvious to my parents that the therapist was mistaken.

My parents were dumbfounded. At times I would seem like my old self again, playing and laughing with friends. Other times I was withdrawn and full of fear and panic. Hoping it was a phase, and praying that I would grow out of it, they did the best they could to correct my behavior, show me love, and move on with life as normal. Unfortunately, things were only going to get worse. The Whisperer was there to stay.

In an attempt to escape The Whisperer, at around nine years old, I began abusing my very first drug of choice. Food. Every day was the same routine. I'd get home from school, sit down in front of the television, binge eat large quantities of food, and tune myself out. I would often eat until my stomach ached. It wasn't abnormal for me to cook myself an entire family size box of macaroni and cheese and eat the entire thing in one sitting. I'd wash it down with a tall glass or two of milk and follow it up with something sweet. A couple of hours later, I would eat again, filling up on the dinner that my mom had prepared. At night before bed, I would binge eat again. I loved being full and I craved the feeling of sedation I would get after a binge. Stuffing myself was the only thing that calmed my nerves. My weight began to creep up, and by age ten, I was uncomfortably chunky. I had chubby cheeks that made me look even more overweight. The more I gained, the worse I felt about myself. The worse I felt about myself, the more I was convinced that The Whisperer was right.

2.

The Limerick

There once was a girl named Shelly.
She sure ate a lot of jelly.
She ate her cat
And she got fat
And her mom said, "Oh, what a belly."

I wrote a limerick in the fifth grade that earned me two gold stars from my teacher, Mrs. Petersen. I was painfully shy, and when she asked me stand up and read it in front of the whole class, my chubby cheeks flushed bright red. My quiet voice shook as I read the poem and sat back down in my chair as quickly as I could.

"Psst . . . Hey, tubby . . . What rhymes with Shelly?"

Mrs. Petersen presented the limerick to my parents at the next parent-teacher conference.

"Very clever! This one has a real talent for writing, doesn't she?" my dad asked while rustling the hair on my head with his hand. I smiled at him beaming with pride because he believed I had writing talent. And that was it. After reading that silly little limerick, my dad was convinced that I was going to grow up to be a professional writer.

Not long after that parent-teacher conference, my dad came home from one of his business trips toting a brand-new electric typewriter and a bundle of white copy paper. "Here you go, kiddo. This is to help you get started on your writing career," he said, handing the magnificent machine to me.

Immediately I went to work. Sometimes locking myself away in my bedroom for hours at a time, I pecked at the keys with a frenzied determination. There was something satisfying about sliding a fresh piece of paper in and rolling it into just the right position. I loved the smell of fresh ink and the snapping noise the keys made as my thoughts came to life on the paper in front of me. My favorite things to write were short and humorous Shel Silverstein-type poems. From time to time, I would emerge victorious from my bedroom, flinging the door open with paper in hand. I would stand next to my dad and watch him intently as he slowly and carefully read every word of my latest creation. Dad would let out a deep belly laugh and say, "This is good one, kiddo. You are very gifted."

It became evident early on that my strengths and talents did not lie in athletics. To be perfectly honest, I've never really needed obstacles like stairs or ice to take a good tumble. There was a short career in softball, and then at about nine years old, I tried gymnastics. During the awards presentation at one of my competition meets, I didn't end up taking home so much as a participation ribbon. Later that day, Kari and Heather crafted me a huge first-place ribbon out of some construction paper. They presented it to me to cheer me up.

After an unfortunate Fourth of July parade incident while playing the flute with the school marching band, musical instruments and marching were also crossed off the list. Especially while doing both at the same time.

I had finally found something I could feel good about. Writing had become my thing.

3.

Ken & Malibu Barbie

In 1987, my family packed up and said goodbye to Minnesota's simple life forever. My dad's new position as senior vice president of a retail chain moved us to Orange County, California. In an instant, we were catapulted out of the practical world of long johns and moon boots and landed smack dab in the center of tan lines and flip-flops. Towering palm trees lined up like soldiers alongside the highway, and an unfamiliar aroma of salty ocean air filled my nose. Sunbathers with bleached-blond hair and browned skin packed long sandy beaches. The aqua-blue water stretched out into eternity, dotted with surfers waiting to catch a wave to shore. Somehow, the sun seemed brighter and warmer than it did back in the Midwest.

Our new house was much different than the more modest home we were used to. Tucked away in the Yorba Linda Hills, it was a large, cream-colored stucco with a Spanish tile roof. Like many of the other homes in our neighborhood, off the back deck was a big swimming pool and Jacuzzi. The large windows and open floor plan was inviting, and six bedrooms gave plenty of space for everyone to have their own room. Sharing rooms with siblings became a thing of the past. The neighborhood was set on a steep hill, and just down the street were two other large

Latter-day Saint families. We were excited to have neighbors who we had so much in common with.

The first time I walked into Bernardo Yorba Junior High, like Dorothy, I knew I wasn't in Kansas anymore. The other kids seemed to have stepped out of fashion magazines instead of school buses. Money appeared to drip off them as they cheerfully decorated their lockers and stood in tight circles talking about their summers. Phrases like "vacationed in London" and "went shopping in Italy" fell from perfectly glossed lips. I was obviously underdressed, and like a Martian on a new planet, it was clear that I didn't belong. Panic struck fear into my heart, and the demons that lived in my mind began a noise campaign.

"Everyone can see you don't belong here. I mean, look at you . . . you're fat . . . and you're gross."

I was already chubby, awkward, and insecure. To make matters worse, I was now surrounded by Kens and Malibu Barbies.

The anxiety I felt at school became unbearable. Because I was new and felt incredibly inferior, I had a difficult time making friends. An obvious rigid social structure existed, and I didn't understand the blueprints. Lunchtime was the most intimidating battlefield of all. As my morning classes dragged on, I would watch the clock with dread. The lunch bell would inevitably ring, and I watched as the other kids enthusiastically strolled toward the quad, picking up friends along the way. Kids would fill the lunch tables with what seemed to be predetermined seating assignments, and I was never given one. I would often eat my lunch while walking around to avoid looking like I didn't have anyone to sit with. Those forty minutes felt like forever.

Because I believed that there was something fundamentally wrong with me, I carried around an incredible amount of shame about not fitting in. That shame kept me totally isolated. I didn't want to be exposed for being any more broken than my parents already believed I was. With no explanation for my resistance to go to school, my behavior appeared defiant. I knew I was letting them down, so I felt stuck between forcing myself to go and the panic that being at school would bring.

Determined to try to fit in, I began restricting my food. Starving myself, I quickly lost twenty-six pounds and thinned out. The weight loss, however, was short lived. Ultimately, the obsession to eat won out. I caved and began binge eating again. As a result, I gained all of my weight back, plus more. My withdrawn behavior and panic attacks became so worrisome to my parents that I was finally admitted into a children's psych ward for observation and a mental health evaluation.

"You know they think you're crazy, don't you? Why can't you just be normal?"

After several weeks, I was sent home from the hospital with a diagnosis of depression and a prescription for Prozac. It didn't take long to see that the medication wasn't effective, and my parents eventually had me stop taking it. They were extremely frustrated that seeking professional help seemed to hold no answers. They were at a total loss, with no idea of how to help me.

A deep hopelessness began to settle into my psyche. Everything The Whisperer had been telling me was true. I was too broken to be fixed, and that meant that I was most definitely unlovable.

In order to keep moving forward, my mind transitioned into emotional survival mode. Being a "good girl" and making responsible choices no longer mattered to me. No one was coming to save me, and the monsters in my head were only getting louder.

"Bruce, sit down!" my mom yelled.

My dad stood there with his finger pointed in Kari's face. His eyes were wild, and he was red with anger.

"You're on thin ice, sister!" he barked, daring her to respond.

Kari rolled her eyes and let out a loud sigh.

"Don't you roll your eyes at me, missy!" he said, leaning forward threateningly.

Just then, my younger brother Brian, who was sitting next to me on the couch, began to cry. I put my arm around him and whispered that it was going to be okay.

"Bruce, calm down!" my mom said.

"She's going to apologize to me or else!" Dad said, gritting his teeth.

"Or else what?" Kari asked.

"Or else I'm going to clean your clock!"

Lately, a shadow of tension and hostility had crept into our home, turning it into a virtual war zone. My mental health concerns took a sudden backseat as our happy little family had become anything but. Screaming matches were exploding on a regular basis, increasing in frequency and intensity with one common denominator—my dad.

The old, fun Dad who wanted to take us camping and sit around with his guitar singing folk songs had been replaced by an angry stranger who had little patience for anything, especially smart-mouthed teenagers. With the new job, Dad had begun going out of town on business more frequently. He was gone a lot of the time. When he was home, he was often impatient and angry. Activities that were once considered as important as breathing, like attending church, family prayer, and spending time together had faded away. It was strange how our church-centered life, which had been such a big part of who we were, ended almost overnight. God, it seemed, had slipped down in importance on the family totem pole. Attitude and the amount of time spent at home were not the only changes in Dad. He had traded in his Jeep Wagoneer for a silver Porsche and a Harley Davidson with orange and yellow flames painted along the gas tank.

Altercations between my dad and Kari became the norm. At times these incidents were violent, and he became physically abusive. His temper was terrifying and unpredictable. As a child, witnessing my father lose control was a lot like watching a silverback gorilla set loose in the house.

His anger wasn't just limited to my sister Kari. Violent arguments between my mom and Dad were also becoming commonplace. They fought about everything—money, Dad being gone, the kids. Threats of divorce began to sound more like promises to those of us forced to live in the center of the battlefield. Only when he was out of town did there seem to be a reprieve from all of the arguing. Sadly, Dad coming home from a business trip became a dreaded countdown.

My family was a mess. Kindness and patience were getting harder to find. The church hymn "Love at Home" was often sung under breath with a heavy dose of sarcasm and eye rolling. The battlefield spread from our parents to the children, and we began fighting with each other more often. We became skilled brawlers. In order to survive, one had to be quick-witted with a razor tongue, and we had to learn to take a punch without crying.

I was trapped. Cornered on one side by the raging battle within my family, and ambushed on the other by The Whisperer, who was giving me the constant play-by-play of my worthlessness. Sometimes all I could do was put both hands over my ears, squeeze my eyes shut, and scream at the top of my lungs.

4.

Patrick

"Here, let me show you again," Patrick said as he teasingly snatched the workbook out of my hand. He was trying to walk me through a pre-algebra math problem.

I watched him as he crossed things out, divided numbers, and moved variables from one side of the page to the other.

"Okay, so X equals 4. Did you see how I did that?" he asked.

Math was not my best subject. With what I understood from his explanation, he may as well have been speaking Latin. Besides, I was too busy thinking about how cute he looked when he concentrated to pay attention.

"No, not really," I said with a big grin on my face.

Patrick let out a sigh and smiled. He smacked me lightly on the top of my head with my notebook.

"Forget it," Patrick said.

He flung the book across the room like a Frisbee.

"Let's just go jump in the pool."

At thirteen years old, in the midst of all the emotional challenges and family chaos that had become my life, there was one bright spot—Patrick.

As a sophomore, Patrick was three years older than I was. He wrestled for the high school wrestling team, had unkempt brown hair, and struggled with periodic bouts of acne. Patrick was unusually intelligent, and because of this, his teachers often had a difficult time keeping him interested at school. He was socially awkward, and he would become nervous and uncomfortable in large groups of people. I found his shy demeanor endearing, and as far as I was concerned, he was absolutely perfect.

Because he was comfortable around me, I saw more of the real Patrick than most people. He was incredibly funny with a dry sense of humor, so hanging out with him always included a lot of laughing. I played along and basked in the attention when he would tease me almost constantly, always with a twinkle in his eye. We hung out in the pool, destroyed the kitchen with random baking projects, and stayed up late watching low-budget horror movies and MTV.

My weight and insecurities never seemed to bother Patrick. I felt that he liked me just as I was. While the age difference was a big enough gap that it kept us from becoming an official couple, one night Patrick leaned in and gave me my first kiss. It was magical.

My time spent hanging out with Patrick was like standing in the eye of a hurricane. When I was focused on him, I forgot about the storm raging all around me.

One Saturday morning while I was doing my chores, my father came upstairs and asked me to turn the vacuum off. He stood defeated, with his head down and a look of sorrow on his face. I had never seen him like that before. I watched in shock as the man who had always seemed to strong started to cry.

"Kiddo, I've made some terrible mistakes. I need you to know that I met with the bishop and stake president. I am being excommunicated from the Church."

"For what?" I asked.

"Well," Dad said, looking uncomfortable and trying to choose his words carefully, "I made some . . . sinful moral decisions, and I don't know what's going to happen between me and your mother," he said. He was sobbing now.

I was only thirteen years old, but I knew exactly what he was saying. Despite what he may have thought, I was anything but surprised. He was telling me that he had been cheating on my mother.

My hand was still holding the vacuum as he hugged me, crying.

"He doesn't care about you. He doesn't care about this family."

"Yeah, well, game on," I whispered back, wiping the tears from my eyes.

Three days later, I talked two neighbor boys into stealing their family Suburban and leaving the state of California with me. At twelve and thirteen years old, not one of us had any real driving experience. As we headed for the interstate, the car phone began to ring inside the vehicle. We'd been found out. We disconnected it and continued our adventure onto the open road. We were heading for southern Utah.

The car windows were down, and the hot desert air was blowing in my hair. My first grand theft auto was in progress, and I had never felt freer. I figured if I couldn't shut The Whisperer up, I'd try outrunning him.

5.

The Beast

By 1989, our wounded family had pulled up stakes and moved north to the San Francisco Bay area. Sadly, it had come out that not only had my father been participating in multiple affairs, he was also accused of sexually harassing a coworker and was subsequently fired from his job. Almost immediately after we moved, my mother caught my father cheating again with yet another woman. Disillusioned and heartbroken, she made the decision to leave him for good.

After years of living in the midst of the noisy battlefield, my parents finally laid down their weapons, and the war was over. My dad packed up his things and left. An eerie quiet settled over our home. I had watched my father make destructive choices that ended in him losing everything that mattered to him. He lost his church membership, his career, and ultimately, he lost his family. I felt a deep sadness for his grief, and my heart broke for him as he ventured out into the world alone. While I couldn't understand why he had made such hurtful decisions, he was my dad, and I loved him anyway.

After my father was excommunicated, he became inactive in the Church and fell further away. I believe my father loved the gospel and thought that one day he would work through the repentance process and become a full member again. But because he believed he had time, unfortunately, he didn't act on that desire with any urgency.

Not long after my father's double life was exposed, my mother had a fallout with our local church leadership and became resentful toward the Church. Her hurt feelings proved too much for her to overcome. After more than twenty years of being a member, my mother also walked away from the Church.

Just like that, in less than a few short months, God was all but erased out of our daily lives. At sixteen years old, my sister Heather remained the only active member of the Church in our home. She watched as her entire family turned away from the gospel that had shaped our lives. I wouldn't understand how painful that time was for her or appreciate the significance of the decision she made to stay active until much, much later.

Our little boat in the ocean had snapped its anchor and was now at the mercy of the storm. We were all swirling in the darkness.

During this time, my relationship with my mother began to deteriorate. Even though I had struggled emotionally for years now and had begun making reckless choices, I had always been soft spoken and polite to my mother. Without any warning, my attitude and behavior had shifted to rude and openly defiant. Desperate for the emotional relief I wasn't getting, I was becoming bitter, and my mother was standing in the direct line of fire.

In an effort to seek validation and get help, I had begun trying to communicate what I was experiencing, but my attempts were unsuccessful. No matter how many ways I put it or how many times I said it, she didn't seem to grasp the gravity of what I was saying. Inside, I was frantic for her to see that there were monsters in my head, and I needed her to make them stop.

Every time I tried to reach out to her, I almost always got the same response: "I'm sorry, Kelly. I just don't know how to help you."

I wanted to shake her and scream, "Can't you see I'm on fire, Mom? I'm burning alive right in front of you! You have to help me!"

Misunderstanding my outrageous behavior as being the signs of an adrenaline junky who just needed an outlet, she once offered to pay for me to get skydiving lessons as a solution to my behavior problems.

Yeah, good idea, Mom. Only let's leave out the parachute, I thought.

She truly wanted to help, but we were trapped in an impossible situation. The hard reality was that she couldn't save me from what I was experiencing. We didn't understand at the time that my problems were beyond the help of any human power. They were symptoms of a disease we knew nothing about and weren't even aware that I had. Those frustrating and unproductive conversations left me feeling even more desperate. I'd often walk away with an overwhelming urge to literally bang my head against the wall.

Finally, I gave up seeking rescue from her or anyone else, and I went out to find a way to save myself.

At fourteen years old, I knew I was onto something the moment alcohol touched my lips. During the summer of '89, I was invited to a party, and a large bottle of tequila was the guest of honor. After drinking that first shot, a warm tingling sensation spread through my body. Calm washed over me. The anxiety I had carried for all those years melted away in an instant. My body finally relaxed, and for the first time in longer than I could remember, I felt like I was okay. I realized that drinking was an escape from The Whisperer. It was an epiphany for me. When I was drinking, I was free.

I drank enough tequila that night to give myself alcohol poisoning and experience a partial blackout. Once I started drinking, I had no "off" switch. I drank until I was completely obliterated. Time seemed to end until, in a hazy fog, I can remember being handcuffed and put into the back of a police car. The cops had busted our party, and all underage drinkers were carted off to the police station to await a ride home from their angry parents.

When one of the officers called my home, they found out that my mom was out of town, and the only one available to pick me up was my seventeen-year-old sister, Heather. While sitting at the police station waiting for my ride, I began uncontrollably throwing up all over myself. By the time Heather showed up to bring me home, I had passed out on the table face first in my own vomit.

After I was released into Heather's custody, I still had nausea so intense that I had to hang my head out of the car window all the way home. She got me into the house, undressed me, and patiently helped me into the bathtub. After washing the vomit out of my hair, she helped me dress in pajamas and put me to bed.

My choosing to drink that one night in the summer of 1989 changed my life's course forever. I had rung a bell that couldn't be unrung. The ruthless craving that is experienced by alcoholics and addicts had begun for me. For some addicts, it may take years of substance abuse before the disease takes hold over one's willpower. That was not the case for me. Addiction had a vice grip on me the very first time I put alcohol into my system.

Being young and naive, I had no way to predict the devastating ripple effect that I had just set into motion. The wave of destruction that began that night was going to span across decades. It would leave a path of carnage in many lives, not just my own. By drinking, I had momentarily found a way to quiet the punishing voice of The Whisperer. But I had no idea that in doing so, I had just awakened The Beast.

That night, while lying in bed with my hand on the wall trying to stop the room from spinning, I only had one thought: *More. I want more.*

If I'd had a crystal ball that night, I would have seen more than the many excruciating years of addiction that lay ahead. I would have seen that the pattern of Heather coming to my rescue was also just beginning. The future would have shown years of her life dedicated to fighting for her mentally ill, drug addicted sister.

Despite her many heroic efforts and countless prayers, she would have to watch helplessly as I self-destructed. Then one day, almost twenty-five years from that night, Heather would finally join the others and let me go. She was going to be forced to walk away from the sister she fought so hard for and do the only thing left she could do—become a mother to my children.

6.

The Thorazine Shuffle

By the time the summer ended, I was officially on the hunt. The beginning of my freshman year started with a complete Kelly makeover. I ripped down all my Whitney Houston and Debbie Gibson posters and plastered my walls with Guns N' Roses, Pink Floyd, and Metallica. I started shaving my head and dying what was left of my hair every color in the rainbow. Thick black eyeliner dimmed my bright eyes, and flannel shirts and combat boots replaced my previous conservative pastel wardrobe. I had instinctively created a protective barrier between the outside world and me. I had put on a mask that I could hide behind.

Even though I had a difficult time moving away from Patrick and missed him, I liked the Bay Area, and I made friends fast. My new friends were down-to-earth, into music, and unusually street smart. Most important, just like me, they liked to have fun on the edge.

Berkeley, with its infamous Telegraph Avenue and People's Park, became our playground. While most teenagers were worrying about their grades or trying out for the cheerleading squad, my friends and I were ditching school and taking the Bay Area Rapid Transit into the city. We discovered head shops, got piercings and tattoos, and hung out with the local homeless kids. I went to parties in San Francisco and time-warped at the midnight double feature of *The Rocky Horror Picture Show*. I looked for "miracles" at Grateful Dead concerts and often disappeared with friends for days at a time.

On top of drinking whatever I could get my hands on, I began experimenting with a variety of drugs. I wasn't afraid to try anything, and drugs were easy to find and buy. I became a virtual garbage disposal for any mind-altering substance that I came across. No matter what I tried or how much I used, I lived with a constant desperate thirst for more, and there never seemed to be enough of what was around to quench it.

On top of the drugs, my outrageous behavior was spinning out of control and reaching new lows. One night, while my mom was sleeping, I commando crawled across her bedroom floor and stole the keys to her car. It took my friends and me less than an hour to total it while spinning doughnuts in the adjacent neighborhood. Fortunately, no one was injured, although the accident could have ended very differently.

This, of course, wasn't the first time I had gotten extremely lucky during a joy-riding incident. As mentioned before, a few days after my dad announced his moral indiscretions, I stole a car and drove across two states with a couple of boys from my neighborhood. Barely thirteen years old, the boys and I drove from Yorba Linda, California, all the way to southern Utah.

"Have you ever seen Las Vegas at night?" I would later ask my mother.

The boys had to drive while sitting on phone books so they could see over the steering wheel. Miraculously, we managed to make it all the way to my friend's family vacation home in southern Utah without causing an accident. After breaking a window to get into the ranch house, we tried to hide the stolen car. On a hunch, the local Sheriff swung by the house to see if it was possible that we could have made it such a distance. We were immediately arrested and thrown into jail.

The following day, all three of our dads showed up to bail us out. During the long drive home, my dad looked at me with that same sorrow and said, "Kiddo, I can forgive you if you can forgive me." Looking back, I can see that my father was trying to show me the mercy that he so desperately desired for himself. After we got home, I wasn't punished. My dad never mentioned it again.

I hated being in my own skin. Hated it. My very life had become meaningless and cheap to me. If there was an idea that was wild or crazy, and especially if it was dangerous, I was in. I sought distraction at all costs. I wanted to run from every disturbing thought and emotion that came my way. But it never mattered how hard or how fast I ran because, like a cruel nightmare, no matter where I went, there I was.

I still had a passion for writing, but I no longer wrote clever stories about animals and rainbows. Instead, I filled notebooks with long, dark poems, each one more disturbing than the last. The creative outlet that had been a positive tool for expressing myself had become a disturbing window into the inner workings of my mind. Like channeling the voice of The Whisperer himself, putting his words onto paper made the messages even more believable.

Born with a sensitive spirit that cared deeply for others, I always had genuine compassion for the people in my life. But over time, the distraction of my own pain was strangling my capability to think about others or consider their feelings. I didn't seem to have the energy to care about people anymore. I knew I was only thinking of myself, but being aware of it wasn't enough to change me. All it did was further fuel my belief that I was a terrible human being.

"Stupid girl. The monster living inside your head is you."

It had been seven years since the demonic presence had appeared in my head. Over time, I bought into that insidious lie completely. I could no longer decipher the difference between The Whisperer's voice and my own.

"It's me," I said to myself as I sawed on my arm with a steak knife. "I'm the monster."

"Pssst . . . Hey broken girl. Spare them a world with you in it and just do it already."

One day, in the fall of my freshman year, I casually walked into the family bathroom, opened up the medicine cabinet and swallowed every pill out of every bottle. I went back to my bedroom, lay down on my bed, and waited to die. When my breathing became labored, I panicked and told my mom. After being rushed to the hospital, my stomach was pumped. Because of the variety and amount of medications I had taken, I was introduced to my first tall glass of active charcoal. Under threat of it being forced down me by feeding tube, I drank the thick, black, gritty mixture. The doctor hoped that it would absorb some of the digested medication before it damaged my organs. Between the forced vomiting and active charcoal, I was lucky to come out of that suicide attempt physically unscathed. But emotionally, I was a wreck. The drastic measures I went to attempting to end my life that day shocked everyone. For the second time, I was admitted into a psych ward.

On a locked unit with other teens, I was heavily medicated and joined in individual and group therapy sessions. We were quite a misfit crew and were being hospitalized for all kinds of disturbing reasons. Some of the kids had severe eating disorders or problems with self-injury episodes. Others were dealing with brain chemical illnesses like bipolar disorder or schizophrenia. Nearly all of us were budding drug addicts and alcoholics.

About once a day, a "code pink" was called over the intercom. The staff would stop whatever they were doing and help restrain an out-of-control teen before they could hurt themselves or someone else. It seemed there was always someone getting his or her hands on something sharp. Our unit had a small padded room for any teen who lost control. Those who went into the room were sedated and came out drooling and doing what we on the unit called "the Thorazine shuffle."

That hospital is where I was first introduced to the twelve steps of recovery, and at the request of my insightful therapist, at fourteen years old I attended my first recovery meeting. I did not embrace the spiritual program that was being offered to me there. There was no way I was going to give up the only relief that I had just discovered through substance abuse. Bottom line was, I wasn't ready to look for a solution to my alcohol and drug problem, and it just simply didn't matter to me if it was going to kill me one day.

On October 17 at 5:04 p.m., while standing on the fourth floor of the locked mental hospital, the ground beneath my feet began to shake violently. One minute I was standing on solid ground, and the next I was being tossed around like a rag doll. As I stood in the dayroom trying my best to stay upright, the staff started screaming for everyone to take cover. The TV and lights went out, and people began running in every direction to duck under doorways and tables.

"It's the big one!" I heard someone yell. It was hard to believe my own eyes as large waves in the floor were rolling in my direction. I thought the floor was going to open up and swallow me whole.

When the powerful shaking was over, we were relieved that the building we were in had miraculously stayed intact. No one in it was seriously injured, but not everyone in the Bay Area was so lucky. The 6.9 magnitude Loma Prieta earthquake tragically killed sixty-three people. I learned that day that I couldn't even trust the ground beneath my feet.

I had spent just over a month inpatient on the psych ward for troubled teens when my insurance ran out and they sent me home. Fearing that I was in need of more help, my mother enrolled me into a full-time therapeutic day program. By the end of it, and at her utter frustration, all that therapy and medication hadn't seemed to help me at all. I came out of the experience just as hell-bent on self-destruction as ever. Other than making friends who became my new drug connections, all that time and money spent was for nothing.

As time went on, I began to focus on how much I missed Patrick. I desperately wanted to see him again. While we often talked on the phone, it had been a full year since we'd actually seen each other. One day I convinced my friend Becca to steal her parents' car and run away with me to southern California to visit him. Without driver's licenses, Becca and I drove four hundred miles down Interstate 5 to Patrick's home in the Anaheim Hills. Defying all the odds again, we made the entire journey without injuring anyone else or ourselves.

My visit with Patrick was short-lived. After spending less than twelve hours with him, we were discovered, and Becca and I were arrested for grand theft auto. Flashback. I found myself sitting in jail waiting for someone to come pick me up. Those charges landed me on probation for a year, and I ended up spending several days in juvenile hall.

Because I had missed so much school, I had officially dropped out by the end of my freshman year. I didn't care that I was now a high school dropout. That seemed about right to me. Besides, it just gave me more time to party with my friends. My mother seemed to surrender to the realization that she had no control over me. I began periodically running away to the streets for days and weeks at a time. Eventually I would need shelter, food, or a shower, and I would show up at home to recover until it was time to head out for another adventure.

That summer, my friend and fellow joy rider, Matthew, tragically passed away. At fifteen years old, he drowned in a swimming pool accident during a family get together in his own backyard. I was visiting my dad in southern California just after the accident and was grateful to be able to attend his funeral. Matthew's outgoing and adventurous spirit was contagious. I was sad that he was gone forever. Matthew's passing was my first experience with death and losing someone close to me. I had no idea that it was the first of two funerals I would go to within months of each other.

7.

The Abandoned Bus

On September 7, 1990, my father Bruce Donald Johnson passed away from a massive heart attack just outside of Las Vegas, Nevada. Paramedics worked tirelessly to save my father's life, but all of their efforts were in vain. At forty-six years old, my father's time on earth had come to an end.

The crater that was left by my father's death was immediate and colossal. Because it happened so suddenly, the events and days surrounding his loss felt surreal. Just a couple of weeks earlier, Heather and I were visiting our Dad at his apartment in Los Angeles. One sunny day, during that visit, my dad and I rode around town on his motorcycle. He showed me the hotel where John Belushi had died and Hollywood Boulevard. We went art shopping and out to eat at a fancy restaurant in the city. My dad knew that I was grieving the recent loss of my friend Matthew, and he was making an effort to distract me with some daddy-daughter time. Had I known that day riding around town on the back of his Harley was going to be one of my last times with him, I would have appreciated every moment of it.

With so much loss at once, I was being force-fed the cruel reality that without any warning at all, the ground can just open up and swallow the people you love. Two weeks earlier, we were riding around on my dad's motorcycle. Now, like Matthew, he was dead and gone.

The night before his funeral, I went into my bedroom and gathered up all of my writings. The joy that came from writing and the belief that I was any good at it was tied directly to my dad. I couldn't imagine writing if he wasn't there to encourage me. In the midst of my grief, I had decided that my dreams of becoming a writer had died too.

The following day, I watched as people came to say their goodbyes to him. All were somber, and some were crying as they placed gifts in his casket: a can of diet coke and his favorite candy, a Peppermint Patty. Watching their dramatic displays of emotion bothered me. I wanted to kick them all out of the room and close the door so I could be alone with my dad. When I finally had a private moment with him, I put all my favorite writings into the casket next to his body. I swore in that moment that I'd never write again. I touched his cheek, turned around, and walked into the chapel with my family.

Friends and family came from all over to say their goodbyes to the man with the big personality and even bigger heart. My baby sister, Hayley, who was just eight years old, gave a sweet talk about her Daddy, as did Heather and I. Kari, who was nine months pregnant with her first child, sang one of our Dad's favorite hymns, "Amazing Grace."

A few days after the funeral, my family and I drove down to southern California to have him buried at the Riverside National Cemetery for veterans. My father was placed into the ground and honored with a rifle volley or what's traditionally known as a twenty-one gun salute. My mother was handed the flag that had been draped on his casket, and then it was over. The finality of walking away and leaving him there in the cemetery felt wrong to me.

Patrick lived close to where my dad was buried, and he had promised to come to the service. I had watched and waited for him, but he never showed. That evening, Patrick called the hotel and told me he was sorry he had missed the burial. I sensed that something was off. His answers were short, and he seemed cold and distant. He told me that he and our friend Sean were on their way to come get me. I was relieved that I was going to get to see him after all.

After the phone call, for just a brief moment, I got a bad feeling about leaving that night. But it was my chance to see Patrick, and I wasn't going to miss it. I pushed aside the warning and made the decision to go anyway.

Patrick and Sean came to pick me up, and from the moment I climbed into the backseat, I felt completely invisible. They barely acknowledged me. They ignored me as if I wasn't there, and they carried on their own conversation. I felt increasingly uncomfortable and I began to wonder what I was even doing there at all. There was no acknowledgment of the fact that we hadn't seen each other in months, and no condolences were shared about the loss of my father. They both knew my dad well, and I thought it was strange that they didn't seem interested in acknowledging his passing.

Patrick and Sean drove me around for what seemed like hours. At one point, we pulled up to a house and they both got out. They stood in the yard and chatted with a young woman about my age for almost two hours, never once inviting me to come out of the car or even looking in my direction. I felt trapped, and I just wanted Patrick to start acting like himself. I wasn't mature enough to communicate my needs or to demand that I be driven back to the hotel. My inexperience forced me to endure a kind of slow emotional torture that I wasn't equipped at the time to handle. I remember feeling like an idiot sitting there without a voice. I wondered what was wrong with me. Why was he treating me this way? The sadness welled up inside, but I tried not to show it.

Eventually, they brought me to an abandoned bus in a field that they were both currently living in. I didn't know exactly where we were, but I did know that we were more than an hour from where my family was. From the outside, it was clear that the bus was out of order. It was obvious that it hadn't been taking kids to school in years. When we got inside and I was able to look around, I noticed there were two beds on either side of the bus separated by a curtain. It was a mess. There were dirty clothes and dishes piled up everywhere. Immediately, Patrick went to the far bed behind the curtain and went to sleep without even saying good night. Sean told me I could sleep on his bed, and with a hole in my heart, I drifted off to sleep.

When I woke up in the morning, Sean had left for work and Patrick was still asleep behind the curtain. I heard cars zooming by. I peeked out of the curtains and noticed a big highway running right by the field where the bus was permanently parked. I was panicked. I didn't know where I was or how I was going to get back to the hotel. My stomach hurt and I just wanted to be with my family.

"Kelly, are you awake?" Patrick asked.

"Yes," I said.

"Come here."

I thought maybe he was going to hold me close and apologize for ignoring me the night before. Maybe he was going to let me cry on his shoulder about my dad while he gently stroked my hair and kissed my forehead. Maybe he was going to tell me how he felt about me and promise me that we'd be together. Just maybe, he was going to love me.

That morning, I learned fantasies are for idiots. Reality is much colder than my young mind could have ever believed was possible. None of those nice things happened. There were no comforting words or gentle hugs waiting for me behind that curtain. Just a whole lot of powerlessness, indignity, and impatient instructions on what he wanted me to do.

When it was over, there was no more talking. After he got what he wanted from me, it was like I didn't exist again. The shock of having had my first sexual experience and the stress of the hours of him ignoring me took a toll on my already fragile state of mind. I was confused, sore, and I felt like I was going to throw up. Every moment felt like an eternity.

Eventually, Sean came home from work, and in order to get rid of me, they decided to drive me back to the hotel. When we got there, I found out that my family had already left. Like the bus in the field, I had been abandoned. It felt like all my insides had all been scraped out in one fell swoop.

The abandonment I felt by my father, my family, Patrick, and God all collided, exploding into the perfect storm. In a single moment, everything that I loved was swept up and carried away. Everyone had deserted me. I was alone with the taunting of The Whisperer.

"You are garbage, Kelly. Look how easily they threw you away. Garbage."

The Whisperer was right. I was garbage. The truth of his words hit me like a punch to the face, and rage flowed into the cracks of my broken heart.

8.

Fluffy Bangs & Scrunchies

Three years had passed since I sat abandoned on the curb in the hot California sun waiting to die; three years since I put my writings into the casket next to my father, burying my dreams of writing deep in the ground with his body forever. It had been three years since the boy I loved ripped my heart out of my chest and spoon-fed it to me when I was at my most vulnerable. Three years since I waited all day before it was decided that I was worthy of rescue and was reluctantly picked up and brought home. Just three years from the day that shattered me into a million razor sharp pieces.

I stepped off the abandoned bus that day with the concrete belief that I was disposable. Like plasticware at a picnic, I accepted the shameful truth that I was made to be used once and tossed aside. Some insults to the psyche are so powerful they can rearrange one's perception of reality. The belief that I was garbage was absolute. It became the crux for all of my decision-making, especially when it came to the opposite sex. On that day, negative and dangerous sexual behaviors were born.

A deeply subconscious urge to re-create the events and change the outcome of the story took over my life. A disturbing need to prove that I couldn't be abandoned became my primary focus. I began flirting and flaunting, and by instinct, I mastered the art of seduction. I prided myself on my sexual conquests, but more on my ability to walk away without a second glance. The entire process became an addictive game. Rule #1—Always leave first. I believed I was taking my power back. Instead, I was offering myself up at the altar for sacrifice over and over again.

By eighteen years old, I had slept with dozens of men. So many in fact, that I had lost count. Most sexual encounters were with boys around my age, but many were grown men in their twenties, thirties, or even older. I was totally unaware of the fact that I was being used, and in some cases, abused. In my twisted and broken thinking, I believed that I was in control. But deep down, every act of meaningless sex further reinforced the core belief of my worthlessness. That awful feeling fed the compulsion to re-create the entire scenario all over again with someone else.

And so began the vicious cycle of a lifetime.

Because I was often under the influence and willing to put myself in dangerous situations, I became a magnet for predators. Before I was even an adult, I had survived two humiliating sexual assaults. It was as though I had a neon sign blinking over my head that read "Predators welcome."

I was filled with terrible shame, and I had no idea why I behaved the way that I did. I watched as hungry, flesh-eating vultures came and tore away bits and pieces of who I was. Even though I was being picked to the bones, I couldn't seem to stop offering myself up as the main course.

For those who loved me, learning of my extreme sexual behavior was terrifying and confusing. It was not easy to see that my promiscuity had a point of origin. When one lives their life behind a cloud of chaos, the days that come along holding life-altering damage can sneak by without much notice. Havoc causing sexual trauma has a way of blending in. It camouflages itself against the backdrop of turbulent teenage rebellion and a bad attitude. So many different cogs and wheels were turning in the destruction machine that was my life. With the initial injury lost in the past and buried deep in my mind, it was easy to forget and then be left to wonder where the risky behaviors had come from in the first place.

The lack of awareness was no protection from the continuing damage the trauma had caused. Regardless of my profound denial, what happened that day on the bus lived on inside of me. Whenever I remembered that day, I crammed it back into the past where I thought it belonged. In an attempt to erase it out of my memory for good, I put it in a steel box. I wrapped heavy chains around it and locked it with a dead bolt. There the box sat ignored, and in time, festered to toxic levels.

I came to believe that my virtue probably had less value from the beginning. Maybe I had just been born garbage. Besides, it was too late to do anything about it now. There was no going back. I was only a teenager and I had been all used up. There was nothing sacred left to save and no one coming to save it for. My fantasies of fairy tale endings had been slaughtered. There was no knight in shining armor in my future. All that was waiting for me was an endless line of men willing to take what they wanted and then leave the rest.

Today, I was eighteen years old, and I was looking down at the sleeping newborn in my arms. His name was Logan, and he was perfect. I gently laid his little body on the bed in front of me and opened up his blanket to get a better look. I counted and recounted his fingers and his tiny toes. I studied his face, memorizing every feature. With his chubby cheeks and button nose, he looked like a porcelain doll. His strong fingers gripped my mine and my heart was filled with love for him. I didn't know until that moment that it was possible to hold so much love for someone.

Nine months earlier, I was a junior in high school with freshman credits and was unsuccessfully trying to catch up in school. I had moved out of my mother's home and was living alone in a basement apartment near the school. I received a small amount of money every month from Social Security. To make ends meet, I was working part-time as a dishwasher at a local restaurant. I was flunking out of school, partying constantly, and sleeping around. I was going nowhere fast. During a brief relationship with a boy from school, I became pregnant. When his mother found out, without even a goodbye, she moved him out of state. I never heard from him again.

I was on my own. I was a wreck. Now there was a baby coming.

Putting my face down to his tiny body, I drew in a deep breath filling my nose with his sweet baby smell. He was round and precious and had been born a chunky eight pounds and four ounces. Seeing him healthy and full-term, I was grateful that I had found the strength to stay sober during my pregnancy. When I found out I was expecting, the reality that I was now responsible for another human being hit me hard. Immediately, I stopped drinking and using drugs. Having been a pack-a-day smoker, I quit cold turkey. I bought a book about pregnancy that had pictures of what the baby would look like each week during the nine months he'd be growing inside of me. I learned about when his heart would start to beat, when his lungs would develop, and when he would be big enough to suck his thumb. I anxiously awaited the day when I would feel him kick for the first time.

Morning sickness came, and it was rough for the first couple of months. Every smell made my stomach turn. I thought it should have been called "all day" sickness. But feeling ill and the nauseous passed, and before I knew it, I felt much better. Pregnancy hormones agreed with me, and despite the fact that I was dealing with the stress of being seventeen and pregnant, emotionally I was doing surprisingly well. My mood stabilized and life seemed to slow down to a peaceful pace. I was given a short reprieve from the darkness and chaos I had been living in.

Needing the extra help while I was pregnant, my sister Heather and her new husband, Garin, invited me to move in with them. They were both attending college at Brigham Young University, and they made room for me in their little house in Provo, Utah. Not far from their home, there was an alternative high school for pregnant teenage mothers. I went back to school full time.

The three of us often had deep spiritual conversations. We talked for hours about God and the gospel. During those discussions, sparks of truth would fly in the air around me, and I can remember feeling brief moments of peace. In a short time, my heart felt like it was cracking wide open. Hope was breaking down my brick walls of disbelief.

Heather and Garin owned a VHS copy of the Latter-day Saint movie Saturday's Warrior. I must have watched that movie a hundred times. The acting wasn't the greatest, and the music, while annoyingly catchy, wasn't my kind of music. But the message really pulled me in.

I related to the main character, Jimmy, and his rebellious nature. I too had traveled difficult roads, felt distanced from my family, and lost my faith. While I didn't have a large singing family at home waiting for me, I knew I had Heather and Garin, and I believed that they wanted me back. Watching Jimmy return to his faith, I wondered if I could do the same. Maybe I could go back and believe again. I started attending church, and I recognized the Spirit there. I loved what I was being taught at church, and in combination with the spiritual moments at home, it was more light than I had known in a very long time.

But strong opposition came in like a battering ram.

"You do not fit in with these people, Kelly. You do not belong here."

Everyone I met was nice to me. But regardless of their desires for friendship, I didn't know how to relate to the girls at church. We came from different worlds, and it was obvious to me that they belonged there and I did not. These girls were college students on the fast track to being married in the temple. Within a few years, they would be moving to the suburbs with their returned missionaries. Soon they would start growing large families, driving minivans, and throwing birthday parties with rented princesses and those blow-up bouncy houses. In their perfectly decorated homes, they would have book club on Thursdays. Books, without too many swear words, would be carefully chosen and they would discuss characters and plots while nibbling on low-fat cookies. On Sundays, they'd show up at church, shiny and perfect. The family would wear color-coordinated outfits, and children would sit next to them on the benches, lined up like Russian nesting dolls.

The world I came from didn't have book clubs or low-fat cookie baking contests. Looking around at church on Sunday, I didn't see anyone else eighteen, unwed, and pregnant. None of the other girls had tattoos or cutting scars. I had a hard time imagining any of these girls spending weeks in a psych ward for depression or running away to live on the streets and use drugs with guys named Dragon and Shorty.

I didn't know anything about scrapbooking, but I knew how much acid was going for on the streets in Berkeley. I had no idea how to give an opening prayer in sacrament meeting, but I could show you how to tare a drug scale. Wedding shower registries were foreign to me, but I could find nitrous oxide at a Grateful Dead show and show you how to use it without falling down and hurting yourself.

I couldn't be more different from these girls. They were all sweet, and they blushed when they talked about kissing their boyfriends. They all dressed in the same conservative wardrobe. They had fluffy bangs and poofy scrunchies. They volunteered, journaled faithfully, and manifested other strange behaviors such as jogging in the morning before the sun came up. I don't think I met anyone who didn't skillfully play a musical instrument. It made no sense to me when they talked about things like China patterns, collecting cookbooks, and who they were going to meet up with at the single's dance. They actually held sober events for dancing. People showed up . . . and they danced!

Regardless of the differences, their life was appealing to me, and I wished I could be more like them. I was always invited to join in whatever they were doing, and I sensed how genuine everyone was. But it didn't matter. When I was with them, I felt like an imposter. I had cleaned up nicely, and if it weren't for the fact that I was in my third trimester, I would have blended in pretty well. But on the inside, I felt like an actor playing a role. You can put lipstick and a flowered dress on a donkey, but that doesn't make it a mare.

No. White wedding dresses and matching picket fences were not going to be a part of my future.

Then there was the biggest difference of all. It was the one thing that set us completely apart. These girls were all going to keep their babies.

They weren't going to have to become familiar with terms like closed adoption or learn what a seventy-two-hour revocation period is. They would have husbands who would go to Lamaze class with them and then hold their hands while reminding them to breathe. On their special day, family would crowd the hospital waiting to hear if it was a girl or a boy, and all would cheer and hug when the baby was born. They would go home from the hospital to "Welcome Home!" banners strung over their doorways and decorated with pink or blue balloons. They would go home with their babies.

The Whisperer was right. I didn't belong here, and I was nothing like these girls.

I looked at my beautiful baby boy lying on the bed in front of me. My heart was breaking. He was not mine to keep, and I was not going to be his mother. I knew what my broken future had in store, and I couldn't bring a baby into that with me. I loved him from the moment I knew he was growing inside me, but he deserved the best that life had to offer, and I knew that I couldn't give him that.

He deserved a family with two parents, a family who dreamed of having a baby to love and the means to create a wonderful life for him. He was this tiny little miracle full of promise, with a lifetime of potential ahead of him. I picked him up, held him close, and I cried. I knew that I was holding someone else's miracle. I was holding someone else's future in my arms. I was holding someone else's baby.

I whispered "I love you" in his ear, hoping that somehow his spirit would remember my words. I glanced at the clock on the wall, and I counted down every minute I had left with him. Two short days go so fast. I wanted to make each moment last. Soon there would be a knock at the door, and it would be time for him to leave. There was no preparing for what was about to happen. The moment a birth mother hands over her baby feels a lot like she's chopping off one of her own limbs and handing it to someone. After Logan was gone, I cried for days. At one point, the crying caused my eyes to swell shut.

The emptiness I felt after Logan was gone was all encompassing. Even my body missed him. My breasts were painfully swollen with the milk to feed him. I bound myself tightly with ace bandages to stop the milk production, but it took weeks for my body to finally get the hint that he was gone. It took my mind and heart much longer.

I had made the commitment to keep going to church and school after the baby was born, but that proved to be much harder than I had anticipated. The depression and anxiety swallowed me up, and in the end, The Whisperer won out. I stopped going to church and dropped out of school. I left the little house in Provo and went back to what I knew best—killing the pain.

9.

The Oath

I had collected a new neon sign that blinked fresh shame over my head. This one read, "Too broken to be a mother." The sign was always on, flickering and buzzing and reminding me of my disgrace.

The people who were telling me that I had done something wonderful were just speaking white noise to me. I had done what I had to do for Logan, but I didn't know how to believe there was any good left in me after he was gone.

"What kind of woman gives her child away?"

Well-intentioned people, who had no clue what it was like to live in my mind, always thought they had an answer for me. I'd been examined by a large handful of psychiatrists, seen a dozen therapists, and had been lectured by more than one school counselor. My mom had given me all the advice she could think of to help me, as had my older sisters. Other relatives like cousins and aunts even jumped in. They all had their own ideas of what I needed to do to straighten myself out.

I had heard it all a thousand times.

"Life is hard for everyone, Kelly, but we all manage to show up and do what we have to do. Try this medication. See that kind of therapist. Find an interest. You have such a pretty face—just lose a little weight. Why do you have to wear so much black? Stop sleeping around. Don't you have any respect for yourself? Read this book. Don't listen to that music. Get out of bed and do something. Normal people don't stay in bed all day, Kelly. Start exercising. Stop drinking and using drugs. You are ruining your life. You are hurting your family. You are so selfish. You are too old to be acting like this. You have so much potential. It's such a shame."

Everyone meant well, but I was bleeding out from the jugular, and their Hello Kitty Band-Aids did nothing to stop it. Deep inside, I knew their advice wouldn't help me, and the hopelessness weighed me down. Over time, I got really good at pretending to agree with them and telling them what they wanted to hear. It seemed to make them feel better, and who was I to dash their hopes?

There was no lack of compassion for what I was experiencing. Only mind boggling bewilderment over my predicament and genuine grief for my pain. I wished that I could change myself and make it better for them, but I just didn't know how.

I was defective. They would catch on and give up eventually, the sooner the better.

There are experiences hidden in my past that only truly come to light by looking back at them through the lens of faith. Only with my new eyes can they even be seen at all. As I piece the puzzle of my complicated past together, an accurate picture of the strange truth emerges only as I blend the spiritual with the temporal.

While sitting in the bathtub not long after the baby was gone, I had one of these experiences. Like it often did, the emotional pain was coming at me in waves, knocking the breath out of me. My head leaning against the cold tile, I sat there in the suffering. I contemplated life and death and whether or not I'd ever have the guts to end my life.

As I begged the great emptiness for escape from the pain, The Whisperer chimed in instead.

"Choose me, and I will make your pain go away."

His voice was calm and reassuring.

"Where is your God now? He leaves you alone in your suffering? I will speak to you. Choose me."

I knew what The Whisperer was asking me to do. He was asking me to turn my back on God for good, and promising me in return that I would finally get the relief I so desperately needed. He swore to me, that if I chose him over God, my suffering would end.

It seemed so simple. All I had to do was choose him.

The Whisperer made a compelling argument. After all, where was my God? All I ever got back from my cries of anguish to my God was silence—cold, cruel silence.

Sitting in the water with my knees pulled into my chest, my weak heart didn't have the faith to hang on. Tears running down my face, I caved and sold my soul.

I whispered, "Yes."

For a time, in a sort of curious anticipation, I waited for something to happen. But no pain left me, and there was no relief in my choice, only an eerie feeling that I had just unlocked some spiritual door and given the dark one an engraved invitation to my soul. Life moved forward, but every once in a while, in quiet moments, the thought would creep in that I had made a pact with the devil that day in the tub.

The old saying that history repeats itself was about to take on a whole new demented meaning. History wasn't just going to repeat itself. It was going to take two of my life's most painful moments and combine them into a new special kind of hell.

Just a few short months had passed since I made that desperate choice while sitting in the bathtub. Now, I was pregnant again. I was also abandoned by the baby's father—again. Only this time, the baby was Patrick's.

10.

The Best Mother Who Ever Lived

"Richie," I whispered quietly. "Wake up. The baby is coming."
"Really?" he said, opening his eyes. He sat straight up and swung his legs over the edge of the bed.

"Yeah," I answered, giggling at his quick response.

It was 12:30 a.m., and I had been having contractions for a couple of hours. Over the last half-hour, they had picked up in frequency and intensity. While Richie was getting dressed, I turned on the hall light and walked into the living room to wake up my sister Kari who was asleep on our couch. She had flown in a few days earlier from Utah to be with us for the birth of the baby.

"Kari, wake up. We need to get to the hospital," I said.

Just then, another wave of cramping coursed through my body, forcing me to sit down on the floor right where I was. So I added, "We'd better hurry. I think this baby is coming fast."

I looked up and there stood Richie all dressed, baseball cap on sideways, with a bag in each hand.

"You ready?" he said, grinning.

Richie and I had met a couple of years earlier at Bullwinkle's Bar where he had been a bartender. We had become fast friends. He was sweet by nature and was easily the funniest person I had ever known. While Richie was ten years older than I was and already divorced, his sense of humor, along with his tenderness, pulled me right in. After about a year of being friends, we started dating. Very soon after that, we moved in together.

We lived on the third floor of a historic loft apartment building just blocks from downtown Minneapolis, Minnesota. Our two-bedroom apartment had fourteen-foot vaulted ceilings, which gave the space a light, open feeling. We loved our unique urban apartment and the location was perfect. Richie was working downtown as a bartender and restaurant manager, and we were close to my work as well. I was only a short drive from my job as a caregiver for a woman with disabilities. While my family had settled in Utah over the last few years, Richie's family lived close to us.

After we moved in together, it wasn't long until, like clockwork, I became pregnant again for the third time. I'll never forget the moment when I saw the two little pink lines show up on the pregnancy stick. I was instantly filled with fear.

"Just wait and see, Kelly. He will leave you too."

What had happened with Patrick and my last pregnancy was still fresh in my mind.

A few years earlier, Patrick had come back into my life just long enough to get me pregnant and leave. The same Patrick who had been my first love and my first kiss. The Patrick who was once a refuge in the storm of my life. The Patrick who had also stolen my innocence the morning after my father's burial and then dumped me like trash on the side of the road.

Our brief relationship ended quickly. A few days after I told him I was pregnant, I came home from work to find that Patrick had packed up his things and run off to the army. Like Houdini, he disappeared into thin air. *"Poof!"*

When Patrick left, I was in shock. When the shock wore off, anger flowed through me like hot lava. As the painful memories of the past and the present collided together, the mental stress reached frightening heights of intensity.

I was still grieving the baby boy I had given up just a year earlier, and with Patrick gone, I was looking down the barrel at another baby to fall in love with and then hand over. The anger turned inward. How could I let myself get pregnant again? To add insult to injury, of all people, I had let Patrick get me pregnant. I let him use me again and dispose of me just like he had in the past. But this time, he wasn't just throwing me away. This time he was throwing me and our baby away.

After Patrick left, my blood boiled with any thought or mention of him. I hated him in a way that I had never hated anyone. Most of the time, the anger I had was all I could feel. Even with nowhere to send them, I wrote Patrick long letters about how much I hated him. I wrote until my hand cramped, and then I wrote some more. When I went to sleep at night, he was in my nightmares. In my dreams, I screamed at him while he turned his back on me and casually walked away.

I professed my hate for him every single stretch mark I got and each time I threw up. I lived in rage as I searched for a family for our child. I cursed his name during every contraction, and I prayed for his early demise the day the door shut and I watched someone else drive off with our baby. Sophia and I had two days together before I handed her over to her parents. After she was gone, the fury inside of me was like poison in my veins. I held onto that rage like a wild animal hangs onto his bloody kill.

But Richie was different than Patrick. Finding out I was pregnant again threw me into an emotional frenzy, and the fear of abandonment overwhelmed me. Throughout it all, Richie was patient. He continued to reassure me that he wasn't going to leave. He was going to stay. He promised.

For months I was fearful each time I came home from work that I would walk through the door and find that he too had disappeared. Convinced that I was unlovable, I was certain it was only a matter of time until he figured it out and got the heck out of there. But Richie was going to stay in it for the long haul. He was going to ask me to marry him, and I was going to say yes. The date was set for late summer after the baby was born.

I had spent the last several months preparing to bring our baby girl home. The anticipation of her birth was almost more than I could bear. I threw myself into making sure everything was perfect for her. Her room was filled with all of her things. She had a beautiful crib that was decorated with pink bedding, and over it hung a matching mobile. There was a changing table where diapers were stacked in neat piles next to her aloe vera wet wipes, diaper cream, and pink baby lotion. I had washed and organized all of her tiny clothes, and they were hanging in her closet on little hangers. A fully stocked diaper bag was waiting next to the door along with her car seat.

As we headed out the door, my contractions were right on top of each other, and it was becoming clear that we didn't have much time. Kari was carrying our bags while Richie was holding onto me and helping me down the three flights of stairs to the parking lot below.

"Where is an elevator when you need one?" Kari said.

I snorted out a laugh as I continued to waddle down the stairs. Somewhere near the second floor my water broke. When it happened, we all stopped in our tracks. Things got serious fast as we realized that our baby girl was going to make an appearance at any moment.

"We'd better hurry!" Richie said, and we all picked up the pace.

Kari got into the driver's seat while Richie and I piled into the back. She wasted no time and pulled out of the parking lot onto the empty streets of Minneapolis.

As Kari slowed down for the red light ahead of her, from the backseat I said, "Kari, there's no time to stop!"

She looked for traffic both ways and then punched the gas tearing through the red light and the next one after that.

"I've always wanted to do this!" she declared from the driver's seat. She had both hands on the steering wheel and a rebellious tone in her voice.

"Just get us there is one piece please," I said, laughing and wincing in the pain at the same time.

Less than thirty minutes later, Tabitha came into the world in a big hurry. She didn't even wait for the doctor to make it into the delivery room. Like her brother and sister before her, she was born a healthy eight pounds and four ounces. We joked that, like them, she had been cooked to perfection!

Tabitha was a beautiful baby with a tuft of dark hair that stuck straight up from the top of her head. She had huge, thoughtful eyes. I knew immediately that she had a sweet and deep soul. The three of us spent hours swooning over her and admiring her from head to toe.

My heart soared with love for her. I didn't want to put her down. She was adorable and she was coming home with me. Holding her, I felt excitement for the future.

It was finally my turn to be a mother, and I wasn't going to let her down. Again, I had stayed sober during my pregnancy, but this time, I was determined I would stop drinking and using drugs forever. I wouldn't go back to the way that I had been before. I swore that this child would never know a mother drunk or on drugs. This time, the weight of the sacred responsibility of being a mother was on me.

I was determined to be the best mother who ever lived.

11.

The Loser

The first thing I noticed when I woke up was the painful burning sensation on my arms. I winced as I used them to push myself up. That's when I became aware that I didn't know where I was. The room I was in was completely empty except for a small nightstand and the twin bed I was laying on. I scanned the room for something recognizable but saw nothing. As my eyes settled on the door in front of me, I noticed it had a square observation window in the middle of it.

Just then, over the loudspeaker, there was a page for a doctor. I was in a hospital. I looked down and noticed that both of my arms were wrapped from palm to shoulder in tight white gauze. My arms felt like they were on fire. Like a tsunami, memories of what had happened the night before came rushing in. I was in a hospital all right. I was in a mental hospital. Blackened, muddy waves of shame washed over me, and The Whisperer wasted no time.

"You are so weak and pathetic."

I laid down, pulled the blanket over my head, and started to cry. As I churned in the swirling filth, I was catapulted into the events of the night before.

About a year and a half earlier, our family of three became four when Evie came into the world. Breaking the mold at nine pounds and two ounces, she had a head full of red hair and a heart full of gold. The day she was born, the nurses glued a little pink satin bow on the top of her head. She had the face of a cherub. The hospital staff went on and on about how gorgeous she was.

Since becoming a wife and a mother, I had, for the most part, managed to keep myself clean and sober. In fact, from the outside looking in, those first few years would have looked pretty normal. I had become everything I thought a mother should be. There was a checklist in my mind of what a good mother was, and I was resolved to marking off every single one of them.

A "good mother" reads to her children, keeps a spotless house, and plays tea party with real cookies and lemonade. A "good mother" keeps her children's toys organized in labeled bins, fresh flowers on the table, and always has her house vacuumed. A "good mother" would never let her house get messy, the weeds overgrow the garden, or her children go all day without fixing their hair.

I read to my girls. I baked them cookies and played Barbies until I ran out of plot themes. I made weekly meal plans, shopped with coupons, scrubbed out sippy cups, and sorted puzzle pieces until my eyes crossed.

Since having the girls, my weight had spiraled out of control. Without drugs and alcohol to soothe me, food became my substitute medicine. While not as effective as the drugs and alcohol, the sensation of feeling full temporarily calmed the inner storm. My binging cycle was going strong, and before long, I was at least eighty pounds overweight. I felt ashamed of myself and absolutely disgusting. I repeatedly tried diet and exercise only to fail every time. I couldn't seem to stick to anything long enough to make any real difference. But it wasn't for lack of trying. I'd grit my teeth, use all my willpower, and white knuckle through it. Sometimes I'd even lose a little weight. But before I knew it, I found myself back in the binging again and feeling even more out of control than I had before. I looked at thin women and I thought they must have something I didn't. No matter how badly I wanted to lose the weight, and I wanted it badly, there was some mysterious broken part of me that couldn't achieve it.

My marriage was suffering. When it came to our relationship, I found it difficult to stop reacting in unhealthy ways. That tired, old obsession to re-create the sexual trauma of my past lived on in my marriage. Like a broken record, I pulled Richie in close and then pushed him away again in an insane attempt to play out the sick pattern from my past.

I knew that I was somehow causing the problem in our relationship, but I wasn't sure how. Even if I had been able to recognize it, I don't think I would have known how to change it. Richie was incredibly patient, and even after all of the emotional abuse I threw at him, he rarely lashed back at me. I often became angry with him for not reacting the way I needed him to in order for him to accurately play his role as abuser. In my frustration with Richie's lack of response to my provocation, I pointed out every flaw he had. I even called his natural kindness weakness. All I seemed to be able to see was that Richie was a man, and all men were the enemy.

My life felt like I was running on a hamster wheel, and the bolts on that wheel were about to break loose. Lately, the housework had been slipping. In my depression, I had become too tired to play Barbies or have tea parties. The old feelings of despair had started to creep back in, and visions of a dark future stared me down. I realized that no matter how hard I tried to make things look okay on the outside, I could never escape who I was on the inside. I was playing the role of good mother and doting wife, but the facade was crumbling all around me. Fighting against it with all my might, it was no use. I was totally powerless to stop it.

When the cutting began, my wounds were superficial. The self-injury practice that I had dabbled in as a child and as an adolescent had reappeared. Caught off guard and extremely shamed that I was a grown woman struggling with an urge to injure myself, I hid my behavior in the beginning. At first, I used dull utensils that didn't do much damage, but before long, the cutting episodes were becoming more frequent, dangerous, and difficult to keep hidden. I retired the dull steak knives and began to use razor blades instead. The incidents now required medical attention and became life threatening.

I had been sitting alone in the dark living room for several hours. Richie and the girls were asleep in their beds, and I sat on the couch feeling paralyzed. The severe depression I was in had thrown a thick, heavy blanket over me, and I was suffocating beneath it.

Sitting on the couch, alone in the dark, I couldn't take another minute in my own mind. I stood up, and with the decision made, my feet couldn't get me to the bathroom fast enough. The emotional pain was inhumane, and I had to put an end to it. The chorus was singing loudly. I tried to cover my ears, but the voices were coming from my own mind.

"Loser! Loser!"

Holding the razor in my hand, I stopped and looked in the mirror. Oh, how I hated myself. I felt the relief come as I carved the word "LOSER" deep into my left arm. After I was finished writing, I slashed both my arms open until there wasn't anywhere left to cut. I left the bathroom, grabbed my cell phone, and stepped outside to call 911. I sat down on the curb and waited for them to come for me.

A police officer showed up first. Seeing me there in my nightgown covered in blood, he stepped out of his patrol car and approached me slowly.

"Ma'am, are you okay? Did you do this to yourself?" he asked, pointing to my arms.

I looked down at the bloody mess and nodded yes.

"Okay, just sit right there. The ambulance is on the way."

I sat in silence while the officer stood over me. I watched the blood dripping off my arms onto the pavement below. I wondered if he was afraid to say anything to me. I was calm for the moment, but if I suddenly became upset or panicked, I was a bad hazmat situation waiting to happen. Finally, we heard the sirens in the distance.

Richie had come outside to see what was going on. All the flashing lights and commotion had been woken him up. I watched and listened as he talked to an officer. He was explaining that I had a history of self-injury and ongoing problems with anxiety and depression.

I was triaged in the ambulance on the way to the hospital. Then began the usual onslaught of unanswerable questions from everyone I came in contact with, from the paramedics, to the nurses, and finally, the doctors.

"Did something happen to you tonight?"

"Were you trying to kill yourself?"

"Do you know why you did this?"

I gave them my best one-word answers, but I could tell by the looks on their faces that they were as perplexed by my behavior as I was.

After being tended to by the nurses, an emergency room physician stitched me for what seemed like hours. We sat there in silence as he stitched and stitched and stitched. When he was done, he took out a tape and measured his handy work.

"I just put a foot and a half of stitches into your arms, young lady," he said to me in a stern tone.

My embarrassing behavior was out in the open. Under those fluorescent hospital lights, it was exposed for all to judge. I hated that my dirty little secret was showing like my bottom hanging out of the back of my hospital gown.

The doctor scolded me, "I could have you arrested for assault on yourself, you know."

As his empty threat sunk in, anger welled up in me.

"Oh yeah, where are they going to cuff me?" I shot back at him as I raised my bandaged arms above my head.

The shocked look on his face struck some cord inside me, and I started laughing. I laughed so hard that everyone in the immediate area was now watching me uncomfortably.

The doctor didn't answer. He just stood up and huffed as he walked away.

I stopped laughing, and my tone changed when I yelled at his back.

"Do you think I choose to be like this?"

That emergency room doctor never called the cops, but shortly after he was done stitching me, a crisis counselor came in to speak with me. She determined that I needed to be placed on a seventy-two-hour hold in the psych ward for suicide watch.

"Yeah, I know the drill," I told her.

Because of the need for medical attention during these episodes, psych ward visits were becoming more frequent. A new pattern had been born. Every several months, crisis would strike, and I would find myself behind the locked doors of the nearest mental hospital.

Being on the psych ward was always the same routine. First, I was tested and evaluated by psychiatrists and therapists who would throw around medical diagnosis like party confetti. Bipolar disorder, borderline personality disorder, generalized anxiety disorder, major depressive disorder . . . on and on the list went. Each time I was hospitalized, another doctor would throw out his or her best guess at what was wrong with me. Then I was "stabilized" on a new drug concoction, coinciding with my latest diagnosis. I was referred to all different kinds of therapy in hopes that something would help: cognitive behavioral therapy, dialectical behavioral therapy, sexual assault counseling, etc. At one point, shock treatment was discussed.

I spent my days in therapy endlessly sharing my feelings. I'd color with crayons in the craft room, eat crappy food with plastic spoons, and watch PG-rated movies with the other patients. Every few hours the staff on shift would line us patients up in the hall like kindergartners and take us outside for smoke breaks.

Nothing ever seemed to help. All the therapy and hospital stays made no difference. There were times that the different medications I was given had even made things even worse. Eventually it became clear to everyone that if my problem was chemical, they had yet to find the magical combination of drugs to fix me. Because my case was so complicated and I was at such a high risk for suicide, it became difficult to find a therapist who would work with me. I was a terrifying liability.

My husband and family were totally up in arms. Nobody knew what to do with me. I would function for a while, and my funny, outgoing personality would come back. For a bit, things would be okay, and hope would peek through. Then before anyone knew what hit them, I was attacking myself with razor blades and landing in the hospital.

We were left with the mystery of the great unanswered question: What was going to help me? I think we would have done anything—we just needed to know what it was. My situation was a nightmare: A cosmic calamity, and like a car accident, hard to look at for very long.

Suicidal thoughts danced through my head almost constantly. I didn't want to keep putting my family and children through this. I was so tired.

"Someday you will be dead, and this will all be over."

That was the kindest thing The Whisperer had ever said to me.

Richie had stuck it out through all of the emotional abuse I threw at him. He stayed through the mental health problems, the drug and alcohol use, and while still married, the baby I had with another man.

In January 2004, I gave birth to my fifth and last child. After leaving my husband for several months for another man, I became pregnant and gave birth to a precious baby boy. Baby Max and I almost lost our lives when I had a placental abruption that caused massive internal bleeding. After an emergency C-section, he and I both miraculously survived.

Because of all the mental health problems, I knew I didn't have it in me to give him what he needed. Not having the emotional strength for what had then become the traditional two-day time period together, I handed Max over to his parents less than a day after he was born.

Despite all I had put him through, the roller-coaster ride from hell, Richie had, in fact, stayed like he had promised me he would. I pushed him away a thousand times, but he always came back with an open heart, willing to try again. He never gave up. Even though he had always shown a great willingness to love me just as I was, I never figured how to accept that love or how to give it back to him in return. In the end, it was me who threw in the towel.

In 2007, after nine years of marriage, I took my children and left my husband for good.

12.

The Mormon Show

By 2007, most of my family had landed in Utah. The girls and I packed and filled every inch of our Ford hatchback with our belongings, and with Minneapolis shrinking in the rearview mirror, we set out west toward the Rocky Mountains to join them.

In Minnesota, my alcohol and cocaine use had been spiraling out of control. I was either on a bender, recovering from a bender, or just completely distracted by my intense cravings. The drug use and drinking wasn't all bad though. It was serving its purpose as a temporary fix. Like magic, the cutting episodes and trips to the hospital had vanished. I wasn't advertising my substance abuse, so from the outside, it appeared that my mental health problems were improving, maybe even resolving. Though I suspected otherwise, I really wanted to believe that one thing had nothing to do with the other.

The move to Utah brought with it the opportunity for a fresh start. Wanting to take advantage of a new beginning, I cleaned up my act and got sober. Yep, things were going to be different now. I would do everything within my power to make certain of it. I told myself that it was time to knock it off. I was a grown-up and I needed to start acting like one. When the girls and I drove into

Utah, I was 100 percent clean and sober. To prove my loyalty to my new way of life, I had even quit smoking cigarettes.

"How long do you think you can hold out before you come crawling back?"

I swore I was ready to hold out forever.

As far as fresh starts go, Utah did not disappoint. The humongous mountains that filled the sky wowed the girls and I. We'd gotten used to living underneath the thick canopy of trees in the Midwest. The views in Utah were breathtaking and extended as far as one could see. The air was dry and crisp, and there wasn't a mosquito in sight.

Heather and my mom jointly purchased a home for me to rent. The house was on the northeast side of Lehi, not far from what's known as the Point of the Mountain. It was a beautiful area. When we drove into the neighborhood for the first time, with just a touch of sarcasm, I nicknamed it "Pleasantville."

Our home was in a perfect location. We were only a few blocks from Heather's family and right across the street from my mom and her husband Richard. The girls were in heaven, because it took them only a few seconds to get from our front door to Nanny and Grandpa Richard's house to ask for a treat or go inside and play. Tabitha and Evie were nine and eight years old, and Heather had three children close to the same ages.

My employment problem was solved when I started work at Heather's manufacturing company. Her business was growing fast and had started taking on big box clients. I threw myself into my job and began working long hours. I didn't realize it at the time, but I had turned my career into my new drug of choice.

Before I knew it, I was promoted to management, and nearly all departments fell under my directorship. Considering I was a high school dropout with a history of mental health problems and addiction, my success at work surprised everyone, including me.

For the briefest of moments, everything looked like it might turn out okay after all.

It was a Sunday morning, and I was on my front porch swing enjoying a cigarette and a hot cup of coffee. A few months earlier, I had decided that I should probably start smoking again. At nearly three hundred pounds, I was the heaviest I had ever been in my life. I had hoped that maybe the smoking would help me lose a little weight and curb some of the binge eating.

At that moment, I noticed that all the garage doors in the neighborhood were starting to open up. Everyone was dressed in their Sunday best, each with a handful of scriptures. I heard car doors slamming as families piled into their vehicles. One by one, the caravan of minivans drove past me and turned toward the chapel up the hill. I looked down at my cell phone. It was 8:45 a.m.

"Looks like it's time for the 'Mormon Show' to start," I said under my breath.

Lately, my attitude had taken a turn for the worse. I had stopped seeing all the many blessings in my life. The worse I felt about myself and my life, the more annoyed I became that I was surrounded by Mormons. They were everywhere. The always cheerful, always waving, always helpful . . . Mormons.

Here they were—the same girls from years earlier. They were all grown up, and right on cue, they were living their peppy, skinny, organized little lives. Through my thick cynicism, they had started to look like creepy carbon copies of each other. I had decided that I wanted nothing to do with them. In my anger, I even joined a local ex-Mormon support group. There I had found like-minded souls who could understand how persecuted I felt. They understood what a victim I had become to the big, bad local church. I dug a deep moat of resentment around myself and didn't allow anyone to cross it. I put up impenetrable walls shutting everyone out, including my own family.

I wasn't aware that my insidious disease was creating an island, a secluded place where it could do whatever it wanted, and no one would be there to witness or judge. The isolation, combined with the outward appearance of my life looking better than it ever had before, was the perfect disguise. The Beast was tired of sitting in the background. He was getting ready to come out and play.

One night, without thought about the consequences, I went to the bar. Rationalizing, I had decided that I had earned a break. I was an adult. I had a job. I took care of my kids. I worked dang hard . . . I deserved a little fun every now and again, didn't I? I mean, it was just a night out at the bar—a harmless night of fun with other adults and a few drinks. It wouldn't be like before. I was a totally different person than who I used to be. Besides, when the drinking and drugging had gotten really bad, I had stopped, hadn't I? I could always stop myself again if I needed to.

Within months, I was drinking and using methamphetamine regularly. Without missing a beat, The Beast had taken over. Like before, everything in my life began to suffer. Most important, it affected my ability to function as a healthy mother. Promises of days at the zoo or trips to the movies were broken when I couldn't even get off the couch to pour the girls a bowl of cereal in the morning. I pushed their needs aside and was focused only on my obsession to self-medicate.

My recently acquired bad attitude, in combination with the drugs, fueled a tipping point in my relationship with Heather. In a misunderstanding brought on solely by my corrosive negative attitude, I threw away my career without a second glance. Blinded by my pride, I got angry. Digging the knife in deeper, I packed up the girls, moved out of Heather's home and Heather's neighborhood.

I cashed out my 401(k), and within six months, I had wasted thousands of dollars on drugs. Any resemblance of a normal-looking life dissolved away very quickly. I drove us right over the edge of a cliff. Unable to overcome the obsession to use, I left Tabitha and Evie to be cared for by my sisters, and I disappeared into the streets of Salt Lake City to pursue my addictions full-time.

Years earlier, as a miserable young woman, I'd had a conversation with The Whisperer.

"Choose me, and I will take the pain away. I will speak to you. Choose me."

In the end, that is exactly what I did. I chose him. Not so much by saying yes that day in the bathtub, but much more by my recent actions. With conviction, I had chosen anger, resentment, fear, and self-pity. The Whisperer didn't need me to sign with blood on the dotted line. I had reached right into my chest, pulled out my stony heart, and handed it to him on a silver platter. He owned me.

The Whisperer was going to take away my pain after all, although it was going to leave me wishing that I had read the fine print of our contract.

13.

The Hourglass of Doom

I was thirty-eight years old when I tried heroin for the first time. In a matter of just a few seconds, heroin took away all of my pain.

When heroin was in my system, I felt nothing. No pain. No suffering. No guilt. No joy. Nothing. But, like all things that are too good to be true, the emptiness didn't last. My tolerance level for the drug quickly increased. It took more and more heroin for me to reach the same void. Before long, it stopped effectively killing the pain at all. But by then it was too late. I was trapped by the dope sickness. Dope sickness is the name for the painful withdrawal that occurs in the body when the opiates start leaving the addicts system. You see, it didn't matter anymore that the drug was ineffective. I had to have it anyway, because a heroin addict is trapped by an hourglass of doom, and time is always slipping away much too fast.

About five hours after my last heroin use, my symptoms would begin. I would get a runny nose, and the annoying constant yawning would start. There was a building of anxiety as my body and mind recognized the hazard on the horizon. With the start of the relatively minor symptoms, all of my attention was turned to getting high again. If I was out of dope, my mind started racing to figure out how to obtain my next bag.

"Ticktock. Ticktock."

After a couple of more hours with still no drugs, my flu-like symptoms would begin to appear. Hot flashes and cold chills would slither through my body from my head to my toes. My skin felt raw, and it was sensitive to the touch as if it had been sunburned. A deep aching started in my bones and joints, making it difficult to sit still. This is the point where the anxiety of having no drugs turned into frenzied panic. Desperation was reaching its peak.

"Ticktock. Ticktock."

By hour twelve, digestive problems joined in the symphony of symptoms. Dry heaving and diarrhea accompanied the severe stomach cramping. The nausea I felt was constant. A debilitating fatigue washed over my body, making it almost impossible to lift or move my limbs. Depression sucked away my will to live.

"Time's up."

Hour eighteen was the point of no return. I was incapacitated by the depletion of opiates in my body. In just eighteen short hours, I was too sick to go out and get the drugs for myself. At this stage of my withdrawal, it would take the help of another addict bringing me what I needed, and even administering the drugs into my system for me to get better. Compassion is a rare commodity on the streets, and it does not come quickly. It certainly doesn't come cheap. One could lay in that condition for days waiting for someone to show up. Even with cash in hand, getting another junkie to part with their drugs is a lot like trying to get a rabid dog to share his bone.

There was a part of my withdrawal that I feared much more than the agonizing physical symptoms. It was a phenomenon far more terrifying than anything the body can put you through. While paralyzed and lying in a puddle of sweat, in the agony of it all, like with the ringing of a dinner bell, the veil over my mind opened and the demons came.

One may think such things are impossible or just part of an active imagination. Before the demons came for me, I thought the same thing. I wrote them off as spooky characters created for entertainment value or to scare children and the naive into staying on the straight and narrow. Before I knew better, demons were as childish an idea to me as Santa Claus, Bigfoot, or the Tooth Fairy. I didn't put any real stock in stories about the Boogie Man. They were just fables to pass around the campfire to try to scare each other before going to bed.

But like so many other things I have come to find out, I was mistaken. The dark ones are, in fact, very real after all. Like shadowy lizards climbing the walls around me, every single time I slid into the worst of my withdrawal, out they crawled. When they were near, images of carnage and horror danced in my mind. I felt their thick presence hanging in the air all around me. Amusement of my debilitated condition filled the empty spaces, and I could hear their demented laughing.

Once, I made it all the way to day eight without heroin. It was the longest I had gone without since I had started using more than a year earlier. The first five days, with my family's help, I had been lucky enough to spend in a very nice detox clinic. There I'd had the assistance of polite nurses, IV fluids, and Valium to help me through the initial withdrawal. After almost a week of detox,

I was sent to live with my mom and Richard in the mountains of central Idaho. I had been in their home for only three days when I fell asleep and had the most realistic nightmare I have ever experienced in my life.

A demon, in the body of a man, was riding next to me in the backseat of a dark car. My skin crawled being next to him. When I looked into his eyes, I could see they held pure evil. With a smug and satisfied smile on his face, he turned his head toward the rear of the vehicle, coaxing me to turn around and see. I followed his gaze and turned my head. That's when I realized we were riding in a hearse. Sitting behind us was a shiny black coffin. My heart dropped and I screamed. I knew that inside of that coffin was my body. The demon laughed at my horror.

I called Heather, sobbing. I shared with her my experiences with the demons. I told her how they haunted me every time I tried to get clean. Even knowing that Heather believed in spiritual things, I was very surprised by her reaction.

"They are real, Kelly," she said firmly.

She told me there was a way to make them go away. She calmly and clearly explained to me how to raise my right arm to the square. She told me to tell them to leave in the name of Jesus Christ.

As soon as she mentioned His name, rage boiled up inside of me.

"I will NOT say that name!" I snapped at her.

My sweet sister proceeded to cry. She begged me to do it.

"You have to do it. I can't do it for you. I would do it for you if I could," she cried.

Crying along with her, I said, "I can't! I won't!"

Such a simple thing, right? But even completely terrorized by the dark ones, I either couldn't, or wouldn't, raise my arm and say the name Jesus Christ out loud.

I hung up the phone, packed a bag, left my mom a goodbye note, and took off. I hitchhiked back to Salt Lake City and my heroin.

My experiences with demons did have an unexpected positive side effect, one that I don't think the dark ones had anticipated. By making themselves seen during their attempts to frighten me, I began to understand that there was much more going on around me than just the temporal world. Because of them, I had started to believe in the spiritual. I began to wonder that if the dark ones existed, then maybe, just maybe, the light ones did too.

14.

The Underworld

From an outside perspective, I would imagine that one might think my choice of prostitution to support my drug habit was drastic, but in the throes of addiction, drastic choices are all you're left with.

In the underworld, there are no buddies or friends. I learned the hard way that a smile or friendly gesture most often masked a cunning plot or a tricky sleight of hand. On the streets, where the dangerous games of survival are played, most of the players are skilled hustlers and masters of illusion. They are well practiced at the art of deceit and manipulation. One learns quickly that goodness and honesty are a liability. It was game over fast for anyone naive enough to wear that kind of weakness in the open. Predators devour the vulnerable in the underworld.

While I was living out of hotels, every encounter I had was fraught with danger and uncertainty. Money, drugs, and undignified acts were exchanged at all hours of the day and night from one dirty hand to another. No one could be trusted, and paranoia ran thick as people turned on each other with hair triggers. Unpredictable and even unprovoked violence could erupt at any moment. The stakes got even higher as overdose, prison, and murder picked off players like sharks feeding on survivors after a shipwreck. We were all just strangers lost at sea, floating alongside each other in the cold dark water. No one knew who was going to be snatched and dragged under next.

For better than a year, I had managed to keep my eyes down and was lucky enough to avoid any serious trouble. Sure, I had taken my turn like everyone else. On occasion, I'd had drugs, money, and electronics stolen. Other minor incidents had occurred, like the day that a fight broke through my hotel room door. I sat frozen in disbelief as my door flung open and a large, redheaded woman leaped on top of a smaller woman, tackling her to the ground. While the smaller woman screamed, the redheaded woman held her down at the foot of my bed and proceeded to chop off her hair with a pair of scissors.

"I do nails, but I also do hair!" she told her.

I was alone with no protection. I did my best to be careful not to draw the attention of thieves, would-be pimps, and, most especially, the well-organized criminals. My strategy was simple. I tried to be invisible. I only talked to the people I needed to talk to. Most of what I needed came directly to me. I was only forced outside on rare occasion by necessity. For months at a time, I closed myself into my hotel room and lived there alone like a cockroach in the dark with the shades drawn.

Time passed without serious incident. Disillusioned, I thought that maybe I had found the formula for success in the underworld. I had developed a false sense of security. Without any warning, precarious stumbling blocks started showing up everywhere I turned. As if the gates of hell had opened up and unleashed its fury on me, almost every person I came into contact with began to turn on me in anger, seemingly without provocation. Where I had once been left alone and even ignored, I suddenly seemed to have a target on my back. To protect myself, I moved from hotel to hotel, but wherever I went, trouble seemed to follow. In a matter of a few short months, the disturbing incidents were piling up.

Gang members threatened to jump me. People accused me of stealing things I had not stolen. I had several frightening incidents with clients that had a particularly disturbing taste for violence. It was around this time that I began to notice that I was being stalked. My stalker watched my ads online and began following me from hotel to hotel. He called my phone, left presents and cards by my door, and when I drove around town, he seemed to be everywhere I went. To be honest, at first he seemed harmless. I didn't worry much about him until the night I woke up and he was sitting next to my bed watching me sleep. He had talked the front desk clerk into giving him a key to my room, and then he let himself in, sat down in a chair, and waited patiently for me to wake up.

As the months wore on, my physical condition deteriorated. Because I had stopped eating almost entirely, my five-foot-eight-inch frame had become nothing more than skin and bones. I had easily aged twenty years. As the drugs did their damage, my skin became a strange color and texture. Raw, red meth sores covered my face and body, and I slathered on thick makeup in failed attempts to cover them. There were dark bruises from my neck to my toes from trying to administer the drugs into my system. It had become increasingly difficult to use due to my shrinking and collapsing veins. From time to time, large painful abscesses developed under my skin and had to be attended to and drained by emergency room physicians. My digestive system had come to an almost complete halt from the lack of food in combination with all of the powerful opiates. Severe dehydration was a constant problem since the drugs made it difficult to swallow fluids, and sometimes I would simply forget to drink.

My powerlessness over my addictions was sealed in stone the day that Tom died. After scoring us some heroin, my friend Tom went back to his hotel room and used for the last time. A few minutes later, he was found dead on the bathroom floor from a heroin overdose. While the paramedics were putting his lifeless body into the back of the ambulance, I was sitting on my bed listening to the commotion and administering myself the same drugs that had just killed him. Even when facing possible death, I was unable to put the drugs down and walk away. The fact that the same heroin I was using had just killed my friend minutes earlier held absolutely no power to stop me.

There were quiet moments alone when I stood staring at the dying woman in the mirror in front of me. Her sad eyes held haunting memories of ghosts from her life before—a life very different than what I was now living. A life filled with the agonizing words that she dare not speak aloud: Family. Children. Love. But she was somewhere else now. She had tripped and fallen down the rabbit hole and had awakened in the bizarre world of shadows. Her new world was filled with monsters, mad-hatters, and the ever-flustered white rabbit.

Ticktock. Ticktock. No time! No time!

The woman in the mirror was lost. She had no idea how to find her way home.

15.

The Vision

Back in Minnesota, there was one perfect summer day with Richie and the girls. Tabitha and Evie were small then, maybe just four and two. Richie and I took them to play at Lake Nokomis in Minneapolis. After playing in the water for a while, the girls and I picked up our little plastic shovels and started to dig a hole in the sand. It wasn't a big hole—maybe just a foot around or so. Once we had dug down about two feet, we hit something pink and shiny. The girls and I were so excited and wondered what in the world it could be. We dug around the object until we could get ahold of it and pull it out. To our astonishment, there, on this freshwater beach in Minneapolis, twelve hundred miles from the nearest ocean, we pulled out a gigantic ocean conch shell in perfect condition. It's amazing how sometimes, in rare and special moments, life can deliver you the most unexpected and miraculous of gifts.

The streets had become more dangerous. My body was failing, and I had started to lose the will to go on. The exhaustion from the constant running to beat the clock was wearing me down. I was finding it harder and harder to muster the strength to keep going. Every day was more of the same—the crooked dealers, the thieving addicts, and the never-ending revolving door of the vile and depraved clientele. I was depleted in every way a person can be—physically, mentally, and spiritually. The weaker I got, the more vicious the vultures became. They were circling and getting ready for the kill. I wished they would just get it over with.

Desperate for relief, I finally did as my sister suggested. With no confidence that anything would happen, but with nothing left to lose, I raised my right arm to the square, and in the name of Jesus Christ, I commanded all evil spirits to leave my presence.

It was only two days after that tiny act of faith that God delivered me a mighty miracle in my dingy motel bathroom. It was a divine intervention so unexpected and extraordinary that I have had to carefully consider whether it is appropriate to share. I am anxious that my words, written in all my human weakness, could potentially diminish the beauty of the gift that was given to me that day so undeservedly.

After taking my concerns to the Lord and receiving confirmation from the Spirit, I am confident that the angelic encounter I had was meant to be shared. In fact, I strongly believe that it happened partly because the Lord knew that someday, not so far off in the future, I was going to share it with you. I've come to learn that rarely are the precious gems we receive from God meant for us to enjoy alone. I am truly blessed and honored to share my sacred experience. I pray as I write that the Spirit will give me the words to help me adequately preserve its beauty and bare its truth. It was a heavenly message powerful enough to shine a bright light of hope in even the most impossible of places.

Lately, I'd been getting weak and shaky. I sat down slowly into the tub. It had been awhile since my last use, and I was getting sick. I had plenty of drugs, but my collapsed veins made it difficult to get enough of them into my system to make me well. I was hoping a hot bath would help bring a vein to the surface. I started my ritualistic search for a vein. Systematically, I began at my feet, worked up to my neck, and then back down again.

I was in the middle of this process, holding a needle full of heroin and meth, when the bathroom suddenly filled with the spirit of my father. Shocked at what was happening, I stopped and froze in place. In an instant, my dad's big and familiar personality was everywhere. It was expanding and filling the molecules in the air around me. Tears ran down my face as I realized that I was in his presence. My dad, who had been dead now for almost twenty-five years was in the bathroom with me. So much time had passed since I had been in the same room with him that I had forgotten what it was like to be with him in that kind of detail. My spirit recognized the presence of his spirit. In that bathroom, it was me and it was my dad.

He reached out, and like he had done many times when I was a child, he put his big hand on the top of my head. All of the bitterness melted out of my body. In that moment, I became a little girl again.

With his hand on my head and joy in his voice, he spoke to me.

"You done good, kiddo," he said.

"You call me kiddo. I forgot that you call me kiddo," I said to him, laughing through my tears.

I could feel his hand resting on top of my head.

Starting to sob, I spoke to him again.

"I didn't do good, Dad. I ruined everything. Look at what I've done. I miss everyone so much. I just want to go home." I was sobbing uncontrollably.

With calm assurance, he answered me.

"You're going to go home, Kelly. You're just not quite ready yet."

His hand still on my head, I cried and cried.

He spoke again.

"You're going home and you're going to write something that's going to make a difference in people's lives. Your experience is going to help others."

I sobbed like a child.

It didn't matter that what he was saying was completely absurd. Impossible even. I was emaciated, covered in sores, bruised and broken, and trapped in my addictions in the underworld. I was dying. But none of it mattered in that moment, because my dad was there. He was telling me that I was going to get to go home.

When he was finished speaking, I felt his energy slowly leave the bathroom. Little by little, I was left alone again. I didn't want it to be over. I wanted him to stay with me. I sat there stunned by the experience and soaking in the hope that came from it. Like a wall had broken, the emotion flooded in, and I couldn't stop crying.

I played what had happened in the bathroom over and over again in my mind. I was stunned that my dad still existed. His spirit was alive and well. I never had to doubt that again. Not only did he exist, but he was also aware of me and of what I was going through. He was even trying to help me from the other side of the veil.

I tried to wrap my brain around his words.

I hadn't thought about writing in years. It was a dream of mine long ago—back when I had dreams. But I had buried that dream the day we put my father into the ground. The idea that I would ever have anything helpful to say to anyone seemed more than a little unlikely. I didn't have any answers for anyone.

Then there was the big promise.

"You're going to go home Kelly. You're just not quite ready yet."

His message held the impossible hope of a future with my family and my children. I wanted to believe him, but the obstacles in front of me were insurmountable. There were oceans and oceans of distance between the reality he spoke of and me. I may as well have been sitting on the moon without a rocket, looking down at the people I loved on the earth below. I had heard the statistics for people like me, and I knew they weren't good. I mean, really, after all of this, what was the possibility of ever going back? No one goes this far into the dark abyss and comes back. No one. But he said it. I was going to go home.

I knew my dad was right about one thing for sure. I wasn't ready yet. My brief moment of childlike humility disappeared out of that bathroom with my father, and my disease slid right back over my eyes.

If what my dad said was true, and I was going to go home someday, I knew that it was going to take a radical act of God to change my fixed and immovable course. I was a freight train going ninety and running out of track. He would have to do something big, and he would have to do something fast, because I wasn't going to budge easily, and there wasn't much time left.

I sensed there was a terrible breaking point on the horizon. Something big was coming. I could feel it in my bones. There was a mysterious darkness galloping toward me, and the closer it got, the harder the earth shook and trembled beneath my feet. As it approached, I stubbornly stood my ground. I continued to swing the pick ax to my rock bottom.

16.

The Catalyst

It was only a few days after my father's heavenly visit when one of my drug dealers was robbed at gunpoint for a large amount of money and drugs. Without any evidence, and based off paranoid suspicion, my dealer decided that I was the mastermind behind the holdup. The next time I stopped by his hotel room to get what I needed, his supplier's muscle men were waiting for me. For thirteen hours I was held against my will while I was questioned, choked, and beaten. Coming to the conclusion that I wasn't the one behind the robbery, they then proceeded to take a vote. The vote was taken to determine whether they were going to let me go or kill me. The final tally was three to two, and I was released.

After the incident, the impact of the post-traumatic symptoms hit me hard. My nerves were shot. My body trembled, and my voice shook for weeks afterward. I couldn't sleep, and when I would finally doze off, I woke myself up startled by my own screaming. My body healed quickly, but that kind of emotional trauma crosses wires and creates new pathways, changing a person's brain forever. My mind became stuck in a state of hyper-vigilance. In order to protect itself, it began a constant and exhausting search for the next threat. Even though I tried to make it stop, from that point on, my brain was on red alert every second of the day.

Because I lived in the same hotel with my dealer, I wasn't exactly confident that he wasn't going to change his mind one day and clean up his loose ends. Then there was the unfortunate fact that I had to buy the drugs I needed from the very man who had me beaten and held against my will.

But not all of the aftereffects were negative ones. The paralyzed part of me that had been stuck in neutral, ready to give up was suddenly slammed into gear. I went from indifference about my impending death to being motivated into action by my anger toward the men who had hurt me. The bitter reality that I had to continue to hand my bloody soul money over to them for drugs hit me like a sledgehammer. I wouldn't say that I was ready to get off the heroin because of some new profound will to live. I think it's more accurate to say that I was so angry by what had occurred that I was ready to get off the heroin to spite them. But regardless of the reason, as a direct result of that terrifying experience, I was propelled into action.

There was another valuable side effect as well. After decades of giving God the cold-shouldered silent treatment, I started speaking to Him. It was evident that if I was ever going to get off the heroin, I was going to need much more strength than I was capable of manufacturing on my own. It was going to take an act of deity. I prayed that God would create the circumstances to make me willing. I truly wanted to be willing. I told Him to go ahead and do whatever He had to do to make me willing . . . and I meant it.

I didn't believe that He was listening to me. I definitely didn't think there was any chance that He was actually going to do anything about it. It felt a lot like I was sending up smoke signals into an empty sky. I assumed that His response to my desperate pleas was going to be the loud sound of crickets chirping. That prayer felt like a total shot in the dark, but I took it anyway.

I didn't know at the time, but God was listening to my broken little prayers. Not only was He listening, but He was also about to take my tiny acts of faith, combine them with my family's desperate prayers, and blow the roof off my life as I knew it. None of us foresaw what was about to happen. We couldn't have, because until it happened to me, we didn't even know it existed.

I prayed for willingness . . . and that is exactly what God was about to deliver.

17.

Demon Walkers

Going into the most difficult part my story, for reasons of safety, I will not be specific about where the events occurred or the people involved. Also, due to the fact that fear can spread like a contagious disease, there are other details about what occurred that I will remain vague about as well.

I was about to wake up alone in the valley of the shadow of death. But it would be on this final dark and strange leg of my journey where I would finally find God, forgiveness, and the doorway leading home.

After the violent incident with my drug dealer, I made the decision to pack my bags and leave Utah. The only way I was going to get through the painful heroin withdrawal without caving in and using was to get away from my dealers. I had to get far enough away so that I would be physically unable to make it back to the drugs. Forcing the detox process to happen was the only chance I had. I was going to get to the other side of dopesick if it killed me, so I hitched a ride out of state.

When I arrived in my new state and city, I checked into a Motel 6 and began the dreadful withdrawal. The symptoms were agonizing, and the days passed slowly. I thought the misery was going to last forever. But it didn't. The hardest part of the sickness was over in about ten days, and then I slowly started to feel better. I was finally on the other side of dopesick.

But being off the heroin created an immediate and serious logistical issue. The heroin had disconnected me emotionally in such a way that made it possible to work as a prostitute. Without the drugs in my system, I couldn't go through with it anymore. By quitting heroin, I was giving up my ability to make an income, and living out of hotels is very expensive. I was facing the reality that I would be sleeping on the streets.

One may think that the obvious and logical choice is to get a job. After everything I had been through, I wasn't yet capable of functioning normally. I had spent years living isolated and alone in a dark hotel room. While my body may have been healing from the years on heroin, my mind was in shock. It felt like I was wearing my skin turned inside out. Every single thought and memory overwhelmed my senses. My emotions stuck me like a hot fire poker. In certain ways, I had become like a feral animal. I was skittish and jumpy. One does not walk fresh out of living subhuman and then turn around and seamlessly join the workforce.

There were other large hurdles to overcome. For instance, I didn't have any references or recent work history to show a potential employer. I had been living like a ghost for years. Not to mention the fact that my current address was the Motel 6. I had obvious track marks, sores, and bruises. By the time I landed in that motel, I didn't even own any real clothes anymore.

Even if I had been able to miraculously pull off getting a job somewhere, there was no one who was going to pay me enough money to keep a roof over my head. My rent was due every day at noon. If I didn't pay that rent on time, I was thrown out onto the streets.

The challenges ahead of me were mind-boggling. They seemed insurmountable. I was in an unfamiliar city and state. I was cut off from my family, and I didn't know a single soul. If there were community resources that could be helpful, I certainly didn't know how to find them. I was still in active addiction, which included drinking and using meth, but I made two golden rules. There was to be no more heroin and no more prostitution—no matter what. That commitment ended up being a lot more difficult than I had bargained for.

Even after all I had been through and everything I had seen, I was still incredibly naive about the real evil that exists in the world. In the underworld of drugs, everything is pretty cut and dried. Drug dealers and addicts are driven to violent or deviant behavior because of greed or their own addictions. Drug addicts act like drug addicts. Dealers act like dealers. Gangsters act like gangsters. They do whatever it takes to stay high and get their money. If that means to lie, cheat, steal, or worse . . . then so be it. Then there are the men who have slipped off the moral ladder and have given in to their own flavor of demons. People driven to do awful things to others by greed and addiction. That, I understood. There was nothing confusing or complicated in the underworld I had come to know so well.

Unaware that a whole other category of evil exists, I was blindsided by a group of sociopaths that worked together in a pack to target, exploit, and toy with the weak and vulnerable.

By design, these gangs don't stand out. They blend well into their environment. Many have jobs, families, and live in normal middle class neighborhoods. They hide in plain sight. These criminals find their prey in many ways. One of them is by throwing out nets online to catch someone who is alone, desperate, and defenseless. Someone without choices. Someone just like me.

I was caught in one of those carefully crafted nets when a man I met online offered me a place to live. With no other options besides homelessness or going back to the heroin and prostitution, I accepted the invitation. I had no idea that I had just walked into the lion's den.

I was the perfect target. First of all, I had no close connections or outside support. No one would see what they were doing. No one was coming to help. Second, my mind was scrambled from the drugs and the trauma. That made it easy to control and manipulate me. My unstable state of mind worked to their advantage. Third, I was a still an addict and an alcoholic in active addiction. Controlling someone by supplying their drugs and alcohol as well as the roof over their head is a very effective tactic.

The facade of normal quickly disintegrated. It was not long before I realized that I was in serious trouble, but by then, it was too late.

Because of the psychological mind games these men played with me, the world as I knew it dissolved and collapsed. In a group effort, they deliberately pushed me toward psychosis. I was being told outrageous information in an attempt to terrify and confuse me: the CIA was watching me, suicide was the only way out, and the occult was preparing to sacrifice me. I was terrified all of the time. I stopped trusting anyone or anything. My mind raced to understand what was happening, but there were no logical answers. I couldn't understand why people would do this to someone, and I was left trying to piece the puzzle together in a brain that wasn't firing on all cylinders. The fact that I had to question reality itself was the most petrifying part of it all.

These men weren't being driven to their behaviors by addiction. They were motivated by pure evil. I didn't know how to come to terms with the reality that some people choose to become demon walkers. Understanding that truth changed the way I saw things forever. It made everything I had been through up to that point seem like child's play.

I made attempts to get away, but I had nowhere to go, and they knew it. Any effort I made to move on with my life was blocked. Potential employers and roommates were contacted and sabotaged. Eventually I was manipulated and coerced back to them. When I tried to reach out to my family or others for help, it was difficult to explain what was happening because I was confused. My story was so unbelievable.

But what I was experiencing from these men was real, and I was trapped—trapped behind very real bars by their mind games of terror, my addictions, and my lack of choices. People don't want to believe that the things that were happening to me were possible. There were times that I convinced myself that I was having legitimate relationships with these men. I didn't want to believe that level of evil was possible either.

In the black space in which I was cornered, I started to crave the light. I was starved for it. I didn't have control over much. I eventually realized that the only thing I could control was how I was going to react to what was happening to me. I desperately did not want to become like them. In a radical move, instead of hating them, I chose to love them. Sometimes it took every ounce of strength I had, but I started reacting to those around me with genuine kindness.

I became willing to serve and love people who didn't care whether I lived or died. The absurdity of what I was doing was not lost on me. The streets had taught me that saving face and demanding respect was all that mattered. My willingness to do literally the opposite of that made me look pathetic, and I knew it. I realized that these men found my behavior amusing and even degrading, but I did it anyway. My choice to love was the only thing I could do that brought me into the light. It gave me purpose and a reason to live, and so I showed love.

In that dark world, I began to think about God a lot. I started to ponder all of the things I had been taught as a child. Sometimes, when I was most afraid, I would sing Primary songs quietly to myself. Usually, I could only remember a verse or two and some of the chorus, but those bits of songs brought me comfort. When I didn't have one person left on earth, God became my only friend. I grabbed onto Him like a drowning man grabs onto a life preserver. While I tumbled and spun down the pit of madness and terror, I anchored myself to God, because in that hole, He was the only solid object I could find.

One day I walked into a room alone, got down on my knees, and gave the most humble and heartfelt prayer that I had ever given in my life. I had surrendered. For the first time in my life, I was unconditionally humbled. There was nothing left on earth that I wouldn't do to know God. I wanted to be who God wanted me to be more than anything else. I wanted it more than drugs or even my own life. I was ready to walk through fire if He asked me to. When I stood up, I had hope that change was coming.

Later that same day, one of the men that I had been doing random acts of kindness for took me aside and spoke to me. That man's heart had softened enough to share with me an important portion of what had been happening. The information confirmed much of what I had already suspected.

I immediately reached out to Heather. I relayed the information that was shared with me, and to my absolute relief, she was willing to help me. Just like that, my family was involved, and my level of vulnerability shifted. I wasn't alone in the world anymore.

As we planned my escape, we knew that it could be dangerous. We had no idea what to expect. I packed a few things, jumped in a cab, and ran for my life. Heather got me checked in to a motel on the outskirts of town, but we had no idea what to do next. We also didn't know how long it was going to be safe where I was. There were many fearful moments during those first twenty-four hours.

Heather and I prayed fervently for protection and a solution. We didn't know that God had a much bigger plan in mind than we could have dreamed. An idea began unfolding in our minds. The thought came that we needed outside help. Someone who could come and pick me up at my motel and drive me out of town. But who? The Spirit came through strong, and it gave us an answer that shocked us. The Spirit was clear. There was someone specific we were supposed to reach out to. This person lived close enough to where I was to get to me in a few short hours. Someone who, when hearing about my situation, dropped everything he was doing, got into his car and sped in my direction.

A phantom from my haunted past was about to appear right in this moment of my liberation. A wondrous opportunity for amends and forgiveness was opening up. I was about to experience the greatest miracle of my life, and when it was over, I would rise, take up my bed, and walk.

18.

The Tragedy of Winter Quarters

I have heard it said that being angry with someone is a lot like drinking poison and then expecting the other person to die. If that is the case, then a huge bottle of toxic venom had coursed through my veins for Patrick for more than twenty-five years. For almost my entire life, I had loathed him with every cell of my body. I blamed him for marking me as disposable right out of the gate of my young life. Over the years, my blood boiled at the utterance of his name in my space. Because we had mutual friends, the shadow of Patrick and his life was always playing out in the background of mine. Patrick had become the enigmatic ghost of my past. He had programmed me for victimhood and set decades of self-destructive sexual behaviors into motion.

If my life had been one of those dark and twisted fairy tales, then in my story line, Patrick would most certainly have been the Big Bad Wolf. But Patrick hadn't always played the villain in my life story. Once upon a time, long, long ago, when my family and our faith was crumbling around me into piles of rubble, for the briefest of moments, Patrick had been my Prince Charming. He was my first love and my first magical kiss. He was the first boy I had feelings for and the first I ever trusted. But, he was also the first to peel off his mask, bear his sharp teeth, and devour me to the bones. He was the first to demonstrate my worthlessness by using me up, slapping an "unlovable" sign on my back, and tossing me away on the side of the road. He rebranded me a few years later when he deserted me again, this time while I was carrying our unborn child.

An entire lifetime had passed since that day I sat abandoned on the curb in the hot California sun. It was twenty-five years later, and here I was again, stranded at a motel and in need of rescue. After Heather made the call for help, I sat on the edge of the bed next to a pile of old fear and tired rage and watched the clock. For hours I sat there while I waited to be rescued or waited to die, I didn't know which. I listened to the cars driving by on the road outside my window, filled with people heading home from work to families they hadn't destroyed with years of selfish choices and addiction. I contemplated my entire life from the beginning to this exact moment. I had no idea what the future held for me.

Then a knock came at my door, and with absolutely no fight left in me, I opened it. There, in the doorway, stood the notorious phantom from past. In a peculiar twist that was stranger than fiction, and too unlikely to be anything other than miraculous, the person that God had sent to come to my rescue that day was none other than Patrick.

Patrick and I drove for several hours before he asked me if we could stop for a while. He said he had something he wanted to show me. He made a turn and pulled the car into the parking lot of the Omaha Latter-day Saint Temple. We parked, and he asked me if I wanted to take a walk around the temple grounds. It was a beautiful temple, and there was a feeling of peace in the air as we walked together up a small green hill. Patrick began sharing some of the history of the Omaha Temple and how the area had served as Winter Quarters for the Mormon Pioneers as they crossed the plains on their way to Zion. He told me their journey was long and difficult and that many had lost their lives along the way. At the top of the little hill was a small pioneer cemetery, and in the center of that cemetery stood a large bronze statue named "The Tragedy of Winter Quarters." We sat on a bench facing the powerful statue of a pioneer mother and father who were holding each other while standing over the grave of their lost child.

We sat silently looking at the statue when Patrick broke into tears. He leaned forward, put his head in his hands, and sobbed.

"Kelly, I'm so sorry. I'm so sorry for everything I did to you," he cried.

As I watched him in his anguish, a feeling of genuine love for him washed over me, and just like that, I forgave him. As I did, the earth tilted back on its axis and the frozen glaciers that had encapsulated my heart for all those years melted away.

I reached out, put my hand on his back, and I comforted him.

"It's okay, Patrick. It's okay. I forgive you." I repeated it over and over again. "I forgive you."

Together we buried our painful past forever on the sacred temple grounds of the Winter Quarters Pioneer Cemetery. When I stood up from the bench and walked back toward the car, I knew I was finally free.

I didn't know it at the time, but Patrick had been praying to God for an opportunity to make amends to me for years. The pain his choices had caused had haunted him throughout the seasons of his life, maybe even as much as they had haunted me. I had never considered that he was carrying around his own blinking neon sign and painful branding. When Heather had reached out to Patrick and asked for his help, he knew that his prayers had been answered.

I spent those first five weeks of my emancipation living in the same town as Patrick and his family. As I began acclimating into my new world of freedom and sobriety, Patrick and his wife took me under their wing. He handed the keys over to his brand-new car so that I would have a vehicle to use. They had me over for meals, invited me to join them at church, and gave me a safe place to talk about some of what I had recently experienced. Over those five weeks, Patrick and his wife became two of my dearest friends.

Before it was time for me to move on to the next part of my life and my recovery, Patrick would put his hands on my head and give me a priesthood blessing.

19.

The Angels at My Door

After a long and uncomfortable ride on a Greyhound, I stepped off the bus directly into a frigid October wind. I pulled my hoodie up over my head, grabbed my bag, and walked down the busy street in search of a taxi. Even in the light of day, downtown Denver looked remarkably grey and dismal. When I was with Patrick and his family, I had started getting used to the quieter, smaller Midwestern town where they lived. Being thrown into this bustling city environment was an assault on my senses. The loud noises, congested traffic, and sidewalks packed with people made me incredibly uneasy. As I observed my new surroundings, I wished that I could become invisible. I would've been perfectly happy to disappear right there on the sidewalk.

It had been only just over a month since I had escaped my terrifying ordeal. The debilitating post-traumatic symptoms were intense and relentless. Because of the psychological mind games, other than a small handful of people, which included my family, and now surprisingly Patrick and his family, I had stopped trusting anyone. Being around people, especially in public places, petrified me. I saw everyone as a potential threat. I had become hyper-aware of my personal space, and I did not want anyone getting too close to me. I quickly realized that keeping others away was going to be difficult in this new urban jungle.

Lately, I'd been fighting a strong instinct to crawl into a dark hole somewhere, close a steel door, and shut everyone out. Over the last few weeks, my imagination had dreamed up different places where I could live in total isolation. There were elaborate fantasies like a camouflaged tree house in the middle of the forest. I imagined I would climb high into the air, pull up the rope ladder behind me, and disappear into a canopy of green. There were other scenarios too, like sailing far away to a deserted island completely out of reach of everything and everyone.

Inside I knew that what I really wanted was to learn how to live among people again, but I was a having hard time envisioning a day that I wouldn't be afraid anymore. In the meantime, my plan was to be brave and keep putting one foot in front of the other.

By the time I got to Denver, I had been sober for almost five weeks. I hadn't touched a drug or a drink since the day Patrick had picked me up and driven me to freedom. Five whole weeks was the longest I had been completely sober in more years than I could remember. While my desire to stay clean and sober was still surprisingly powerful and intact, my recovery was brand new, and it felt fragile and delicate. I finally had this tiny flame of hope for recovery, and I was afraid that if I breathed wrong, I would accidentally blow it out. I knew that if I let that tender flame of hope go out, it was game over.

My niece had offered me a place to live with her in Denver for a few months. The tiny studio apartment barely had enough room for one person. The only place big enough for me to stretch out and sleep was in her closet, but I was incredibly grateful for a safe place to rest my head.

When the cab stopped in front of the small brownstone apartment building that was to be my new home, I could see that the building sat dead center in the middle of an out-of-control homeless population. There was clear evidence all around of a serious drug problem. My heart sank.

What have I gotten myself into? I thought.

That evening, my niece went out with her friends, and I stayed home alone. Because of the thin walls, I could hear the other tenants all around me. There was a lot of laughing and loud music with the blatant, skunky aroma of burning drugs. Because there was no TV or radio in the apartment, there was no way for me to drown out the noise, and I could do nothing about the distinctive smell of smoke in the air. It was right about this time that I realized my phone didn't work well in the building. Frustrated, my emotions began to unravel, and I started to panic. Suddenly I felt like an animal trapped in a cage again.

Feeling claustrophobic, I stepped into the alley to breathe and see if I could get any service on my phone. Still no luck. Standing there in the freezing cold under a street light, with tears running down my face, I scanned my surroundings. Garbage and drug paraphernalia sprinkled the ground as far as I could see in every direction. It was clear to me that our apartment's back alley served as a shooting gallery. With that harsh realization, despair overtook me, and I broke down sobbing.

Heather and I had prayed for weeks for an answer of where I should go next, and we did not choose Denver lightly. We had both been confident that it was the next step of my journey, and to be honest, it's not as though I had a ton of other options to choose from. By this time in my life, I'd sufficiently burned all of my bridges. As I was looking at the dirty streets, I began to seriously doubt the answer we thought we had been given. Why would God send me here to this awful place? It seemed like Denver was perhaps the worst place a recovering addict could ever go to stay clean.

I wanted a new life more than anything, but I was not naive about the situation I found myself in. I was a drug addict, and now

I was literally surrounded by all of my powerful vices. Bewildered, I wondered how in the world I would ever stay sober in the middle of this nightmare. The dread wrapped around my chest and neck, choking the hope out of me. The hard bottom line was, no matter how badly I wished it were different, the incredibly difficult circumstances I found myself in were totally outside of my ability to change or control. There was nothing I could do about the fact that I was a drug addict in the middle of a drug-infested community. Not a single thing. I couldn't stop it or wish it away, and I definitely wasn't wearing any magic ruby-red slippers.

I stood in that filthy alley with a crushed heart, and I pled with God to comfort me. I begged Him to take away my fear and replace it with hope. I told Him I was willing to embrace His plan and surrender into it with all of my heart, and I meant it, but I needed to know that this was really where He wanted me. If I could know that, then I could be courageous enough to keep going. I was standing in the middle of a windstorm. Trusting God was the only chance I had to keep that little flame of hope from blowing out.

After my earnest prayer, I walked back into the apartment, closed the door, and hung up my coat. As I went to take off my shoes, there was a soft knock at the door. Nervously, I opened it. My mouth dropped open as I recognized who I was looking at. I think I may have even gasped out loud. There, standing in front of me, both grinning ear to ear, were two sister missionaries from The Church of Jesus Christ of Latter-day Saints. I was sure I was looking at two angels.

I invited the sisters in and introduced myself. With the tears of despair still in my eyes, I told them how moments before they had knocked on my door, I had prayed to God for some much-needed comfort. And then, as if they had manifested out of thin air, there they were!

The sister missionaries explained to me that they had come across my niece's information and decided that this was the night they should try to visit with her. My niece had lived in that building for over a year, yet this was the night and the very moment that they felt prompted to come. They were there seconds after my desperate plea to God. All three of us recognized and acknowledged the power of the divinity of that moment. I bathed in the unmistakable and palpable Spirit that was present in the room with us as we talked about it. Moments earlier, I was falling alone down a deep hole of despair, and in the wink of an eye, I had more hope than I had felt in my entire lifetime. It is a moment I will carry with me into eternity.

That night's immediate answer to my prayer adjusted my ability to see the reality of the spiritual realm around me. I knew without a doubt that the sister missionaries showing up at that precise moment was not a coincidence. I had been delivered a clear and glaring answer to my prayer as a gift. That gift came directly from God. The blatant answer to my prayer served a much bigger purpose than to simply comfort me on this one occasion. It was a heavenly gift that just kept giving. From that singular experience, a domino effect of understanding began unfolding in my consciousness. Light switches of awareness were suddenly being thrown on in my mind. Huge floodlights were now shining on the truth in front of me. A truth I could not see until now.

First and foremost, God was real. He suddenly went from being a frightening, illusive, and abstract concept into a loving Father that was literally with me at all times. He had always been there; it's just that I couldn't see Him because I was tuned into the wrong frequency. A thick wall of stubborn pride and an unwilling heart had blinded my eyes from reality itself. It took a desperate leap of faith and a level of humility I had never reached before to become dialed in enough to see Him. When I finally did, standing under the bright stadium lights right in front of me was God.

That transformative knowledge was followed by the next realization. Because of His willingness to comfort me like He had, I now knew I was a loved daughter of God. Not a drug addict. Not a homeless prostitute. Not a terrible mother. Not unlovable.

The Whisperer and a lifetime of his crippling and ruinous lies were suddenly exposed by the simple knowledge of who I really was. The many years of The Whisperer's calculated efforts to convince me that I had somehow been created unlovable were all now in vain. There was nothing The Whisperer could do or say to stop the truth that God was revealing to me through my new eyes of faith. He could not stop me from knowing that I was the cherished daughter of the most loyal, honorable, and loving Being who ever was. With that awareness, all the deep-rooted self-hatred I had dragged around with me my entire life started to fall away. The ugly stigma and shameful labels fell away from me like scales, and I found that I was reborn in new skin as a beloved child of God.

My testimony grew roots from there. I craved the Spirit that those sister missionaries carried with them, and I wanted to have that feeling with me all of the time. Grateful to have two more people to add to my short list of those I trusted, they started coming to visit with me often. They asked me to come to church and to read the Book of Mormon. I did exactly what they asked of me, and when I opened that book and started reading, it was as though truth was jumping off the page. I had been lost and wandering in the mists of confusion for so long that the sudden and stark contrast of the simple truths of the gospel in the Book of Mormon were startlingly obvious. The adversary's distracting horse and pony show dissolved away, and the devil behind the curtain was exposed. Finally getting real answers to life quenched a thirst I didn't even know I had.

As I read and pondered, the dusty memories of my childhood started floating back to me. I began remembering the strong testimony I'd had as a little girl. I started remembering my faith. But it was more than that. An echo of ancient memories deep inside of me somehow went further in the past than my childhood. My spirit started remembering that there was another me once, a me who lived in another space and in another time, a valiant and courageous me that had made a promise to someone.

I was beginning to hear the new voice. This voice was much different from the cruel sadistic shamer that had appeared when I was seven years old. This voice was gentle, and it burned within me like white fire. This voice pierced my very soul.

"You are lovable, because you are my child."

20.

Surrender = Victory

A couple of weeks after I'd arrived in Denver, for a brief moment my disease got the best of me, and I experienced a heartbreaking relapse. As the familiar darkness washed over me, I knew the moment I used that I had made a colossal mistake. Terribly distraught and full of guilt and fear, with a solemn oath I flushed the rest of my drugs down the toilet. Then I picked up the phone, called Heather and my mom, and told them what had happened. To their credit, and I believe being truly inspired, they did not add to the tremendous shame I was feeling, nor did they lose faith in me. As I cried about what I had done, Heather lovingly explained that an addict getting sober can be a lot like a baby fawn learning to walk for the first time.

"Just because you get wobbly and fall down once doesn't mean you stay down," she told me. "Get up, brush yourself off, and keep going, because eventually, you'll be steady on your feet."

Their encouragement and enduring belief that change was possible even for me helped give me the strength to keep going in a desperate moment where giving up could have been so easy. It turns out she was exactly right, and within days of the relapse, the feelings of gloom started to disappear. With each step forward, to my relief, the bright light of hope returned. Before I knew it, days had turned into weeks and weeks had turned into months, and astonishingly, I was still sober.

While I believe every moment of the struggle was necessary and carried with it everlasting purpose, my three months in Denver had been challenging ones. Despite the many difficulties I faced, like a daisy growing through a small crack in a sea of pavement, my unlikely testimony of God continued to flourish and bloom. As the desires of my heart changed and my fearless obedience to God took hold, I became more sensitive to the Spirit of the Lord. Before I knew it, I was perceptive enough to notice even the subtle diminishing that I experienced after smoking a cigarette. Not willing to sacrifice even the smallest measure of my new Companion and Comforter, one day I threw away my pack of cigarettes and quit. After twenty-eight years of being a chain smoker, I was released from my nicotine addiction.

God was crushing my chains and pulverizing my shackles. The heavy iron bonds I had long worn were falling to the earth and into fine dust. I was witnessing the miracles that happen when someone staunchly believes in the love and power of God. Incredibly, I was sober, and there was not a single doubt in my mind that God was the only thing standing between my drugs and me. He was the magic variable to my life-long mystifying and complex problem with addiction. The answer to success was no longer illusive. It turned out that the equation was very simple after all.

Bold Faith + Unconditional Surrender = Absolute Victory

Along with my new confidence in God's grace came a genuine excitement to demonstrate my dedication to Him through small or mighty acts of faith. I walked miles in freezing weather through dangerous neighborhoods to get to and from church, sometimes two and three times a week. Because of my profound anxiety and a painful arthritis flare up, those walks were especially difficult. But God wanted me at church, so I was prepared to crawl there if I had to. My joints ached constantly, and in our little apartment, it seemed there was no comfortable place to be. The small air mattress that was my bed on the floor of the closet leaked air and was usually flat. That meant I was often sleeping directly on hardwood floors. Eventually, because of the physical pain, my sweet niece let me sleep on her futon and she took the floor. I did my best to be grateful for what I had, and I tried not to focus on the struggles or discomforts. Being grateful in Denver was easy, because every time I stepped outside, I walked past a homeless person sleeping on cardboard trying to stay alive. How thankful I was that I was able to sleep safely indoors in the warm air.

My fear of the future was evaporating and being replaced with a quiet serenity. A cool river of peace cleansed my soul as my strong will melted into God's in mighty unity. Every day, even several times a day, I pled with God to show me the next right thing to do, and then I begged Him for the strength to do it. My loyalty was fierce and fixed as I continued in this pattern of surrender. I repeated my prayer often and with sincere conviction . . . Thy will, not mine, be done. Thy will, not mine, be done. I knew the uphill road of recovery was likely to be grueling, but none of that terrified me anymore, because I now knew that no matter what lay ahead, with God, all things are possible.

21.

The Prodigal Child

Tucked deep within the protection of the mighty Rocky Mountains and directly in the heart of Idaho lies the heavenly little town of McCall. Under the shadow of magnificent snow-capped mountains and nestled around the clear water of Payette Lake, McCall is one of those rare pearls that is loved by all who have been lucky enough to find it. As the seasons change, the summer lake homes seamlessly transform into snow-covered winter cottages. Most of the year the air is filled with the smell of pine trees and wood-burning stoves. In this almost magical place, the wildlife step out of the thick forest and casually wander the streets, living in perfect harmony with their human neighbors. Having been mesmerized by its unpretentious charm and stunning beauty, loyal visitors come back with their families year after year to play and revel in the great outdoors.

I couldn't have hand-chosen a more perfect place to be reborn.

Taking a giant leap of faith, my mom and stepfather, Richard, bravely offered me a place to stay in their home in picturesque McCall, Idaho. Just a few years earlier, I had stayed with them, but shortly after I had arrived, the call of The Beast proved too much for me to resist. Leaving my mom with a note, a broken heart, and a barrel of concern, I took off in the middle of the night and hitchhiked back to my heroin. Because my mom and Richard were courageous enough to believe in second chances, my three months of sleeping in a closet in downtown Denver was over.

When I showed up in McCall, I was more than just a little worse for the wear. Because I now had some solid clean time, my skin had cleared up and my eyes had some life back in them, but for a long time I had been living a rugged and transient lifestyle, and it showed. Needless to say, there hadn't been a lot of life's little luxuries for quite some time, and looking in the mirror hadn't been at the top of my priority list. I hadn't realized how worn down I had become by the effort it took to just get by. When I walked into my mom's clean, inviting, and well-stocked home, I felt a lot like orphan Annie did when walking into Daddy Warbucks' mansion for the first time. While I didn't break into song and dance over it or anything, I do remember feeling that I was the luckiest girl in the entire world. Their home was so tidy that there was almost a cartoon sparkle coming from everything. The dogs were quietly napping on the couch next to the warm fireplace, and my mom's house was filled with the nostalgic aroma of something delicious cooking on the stove.

To me, the very best part of the house was my soft and luxurious queen-sized bed. Sheets had never seemed so crisp and clean, and layers of fluffy white pillows lined the headboard. Slipping under the downy fresh feather comforter for the first time was almost enough to make me start feeling human again. With a sharp sting of regret, I wondered how I could have ever been so blind that I was unable to appreciate what my mom and Richard had tried to offer me once before.

In all honesty, though, the happiness and gratitude I felt was about so much more than just the relief of suddenly having many of life's comforts back. I was finally safe and tucked away in this beautiful little town in the mountains, far out of the reach of all the bad people who had hurt me. My brain was starting to wrap itself around the idea that maybe I was actually out of danger. And maybe, just maybe, I wasn't going to live the rest of my life afraid of other people. The possibilities that hope opened up for my life were endless, and the thought of not being scared anymore brought me incredible joy.

But the most amazing part of it all, like I was in a dream, I suddenly had my mom back. Because I had reconciled myself to the very realistic idea that I was going to die, I had given up on the idea of ever seeing my mom again. But here she was, right in front of me, and I could talk with her and reach out and hug her. Being with her meant far more to me than home-baked cookies and fluffy pillows. I had missed her so much. I was very humbled that God had facilitated our reunion. I should've been dead, but instead, because of God's mercy, I was sober and alive . . . and I had my mommy. That first night, snuggled in my cozy bed at my mom's house, was the deepest I had slept in a very long time.

My Mom and Richard were both incredibly patient with me. At first, it was a strange feeling to be around people who were loving and genuinely cared about me. I wasn't used to authentic kindness. I had a lot of fear that I was going to accidentally do something to make them mad at me. But they were both steady, consistent, and understanding while I began to heal.

For months after I had gotten to McCall, I wasn't yet comfortable going into town on my own. Even in the slow-paced atmosphere, public places at times still caused overwhelming panic in me. My Mom helped me acclimate by taking me with her on short outings to the grocery store or even just a quick trip to the post office or pharmacy. Richard would often take us on long drives around the beautiful lake, down to the Salmon River, or all the way up to rustic Burgdorf to enjoy the quiet outdoors and sit in the hot springs. We didn't have to drive very far to lose our cell phone service and be the only people around for miles. We would talk and laugh and play with the dogs. Those long drives with my mom and Richard were healing medicine to my wounded soul. While the process of gaining my independence was two steps forward and one back, with time and practice I eventually got more comfortable venturing out on my own.

As a side effect of being in a space that my brain deemed was safe, bubbling up from far beneath came a heap of feelings that I hadn't processed yet. Because I finally had some mental energy to spare, I was able to start grieving and really feeling the pain of all the loss and trauma. With an unclouded mind, I was also truly recognizing the anguish my behavior had caused others. Seeing through clear eyes, especially what I had done to my children, was a tough picture to view. The future of my relationship with my girls was uncertain. Incredible damage had been done. Our family dynamic had been altered in my absence. While my heart ached to be their mother again, I had to accept and come to terms that my role was, at least for now, one of that of an aunt. The river of loss ran deep in my soul, but I handed over what I could not change to God, and I asked Him for His help to bear it. Certain kinds of healing can take years or maybe even a lifetime, but I had faith that God was capable of repairing even the most broken of relationships.

Many times my mom and I cuddled up on her bed with the dogs. For hours she would listen patiently as I talked about the many things I had been through. She let me cry and grieve, and she gently encouraged me to share. I told her all about my fears, my regrets, and my hopes for the future. I talked about my testimony of God and how it was by His power alone that I was alive and sober. During those months living with my mom, my relationship with her blossomed, and she became my best friend.

When I returned to my Mother, she saw me through eyes of compassion, ran toward me, fell on my neck, and kissed me. With open arms, she embraced me and celebrated the return of her prodigal child.

22.

Transcendent Synchronicities

In the chaos of active addiction, I had become the queen of unfulfilled resolutions. Like living in a twisted version of groundhogs day, I'd wake up with the intense emotional and physical symptoms of a hangover. Feeling scraped of all my humanity, I would swear off drugs and alcohol once and for all. I would delete numbers out of my phone, dump my booze down the drain, and throw away all my drug paraphernalia. As the shame crushed my chest, I would declare that this time was going to be different; this time I was going to quit for good. Then, without any forewarning, somewhere in the world a butterfly would flap its wings. The wind would blow sideways, taking with it the recollection of all of the pain and suffering I had been in only hours earlier. My adamant resolve was mysteriously swept up and blown away. My memory of the excruciating consequences was erased altogether. No matter how hard I tried, my consciousness could not retain the reality of the torment. Then, like sand in my hands, my willpower slipped right through the cracks of my fingers. Before I knew it, like picking up a sledgehammer and swinging it at my own head, I was using again. When morning came around and the trance was broken, I would wake up being crushed by the familiar shame. Swearing drugs and alcohol off forever, I would declare that this time it was going to be different. This time I was done for good. And I meant it, until somewhere in the world a butterfly would flap its wings.

Only ever knowing that nightmare stuck on repeat, a dependable, healthy routine was a luxury I had never had. In order to have hope of a different life, a sober life, I needed to change my approach to the way I did everything. If I continued to live the same way I always had, it seemed reasonable to me to expect to get what I'd always gotten, and that dark, miserable life was no longer acceptable to me. So when I moved to McCall, in order to help ensure my long-term sobriety, I began to construct a solid foundation from the building blocks of small, yet vital, daily spiritual habits. More simply put, I started showing up and earnestly doing my 1 percent so that God could take care of the 99.

Coming to understand that I could only expect God to keep me sober one day at a time, I began asking Him directly for His help every single morning. What once used to only be sporadic and desperate cries to God to save me from my self-imposed mess, had evolved into consistent offerings of gratitude and sincere supplications to achieve His will. Because of this new constancy, and honest desire to connect with Him, over a short period of time, my conversations with God went from feeling awkward into intimate sacred acts of communion. We grew closer together since there was no longer any doubt left in my mind that when I called out to Him, the tender feelings of my heart were cared about, and in His timing, my righteous desires were being acted upon. I was repeatedly astonished as Heavenly Father often matched my bold prayers of faith with conspicuous and loving responses. All those years I had unnecessarily lived in a vacuum of emptiness, and now, to my great relief, I was never alone anymore. Prayer had become my lifeline. I wasn't at all afraid to hit my knees as many times as I needed during the day for increased connection or support. Then at night, I offered Him fervent thanks for another day clean and sober.

I steadily feasted on the scriptures as part of my new routine. Remarkably, the words in the verses came alive as I noticed scripture stories and gospel principles being woven into the events of my life in transcendent synchronicities. As I studied and pondered, it amazed me how many times the scriptures preciously related to a current experience I was having. How often the inspiration or comfort I needed in a moment came directly from what I had recently read. The words were like fireflies of warm light and knowledge dancing around my head, and I could reach out and capture them at will. As a direct blessing from investing my mind and heart into the scriptures, sweet tender mercies manifested themselves, changing difficult moments into peaceful reminders that I was loved and not alone. The Book of Mormon in particular was becoming a trusted friend that provided reliable strength in real time. It didn't take long for me to develop a deep love for the words of the Savior and the impassioned testimonies of our prophets of old. This continual breathing in the truths of the gospel began to revolutionize the way I related to the very world around me.

As I continued in this pattern and my faith increased, I developed an exciting and almost insatiable thirst for more knowledge of the gospel. I was curious about all I had missed during my years of inactivity in the Church, so I began searching for and soaking up all the information I could get my hands on. Whether I was driving in my car or doing the dishes, I filled the air around me with BYU devotionals, audio scriptures, and general conference talks. I searched the internet and LDS.org for inspirational or educational videos about the Savior. It was through watching spiritually impactful videos about the First Vision that I developed a firm testimony of Joseph Smith as the prophet of the restoration. In only a few short months, I had listened to every conference talk from the 1970s up to the present day. A genuine love had grown in my heart for our modern-day prophets and apostles.

I had been parched and wandering aimlessly in a barren desert. Finally hearing and experiencing the sweet and delicious truths quenched my bone-dry soul through and through. The Spirit penetrated my bosom to its very core and whispered firmly in my ear.

"This is truth."

In addition to daily practices, I needed to add other important changes to my life as well. As I drove up to the chapel for my first sacrament meeting in the McCall Second Ward, I was so scared that I was shaking. Part of me wanted to turn the car around, go home, and climb back into bed. I seriously wondered if I would fit in or what people would think if they got to know me or the unsavory details of my life. Would I feel too different or judged and then not want to come back? Would people see beyond my colorful history and love me just as I am, flaws and all? Old memories of perfect girls with poofy bangs and scrunchies floated through my head, and right on cue, The Whisperer chimed in with his tired declarations that I didn't belong. But this time, I pushed aside the old stale feelings of inferiority, and I didn't run away. Instead, I turned to God for His help.

Right before I walked inside the church building, I said a small prayer and asked Heavenly Father to help me have courage. I got the strong impression that I was not there necessarily to get something but that I was there to give and share my love with others. The thought came to me that maybe some people were going to judge me for the life I had led, and maybe that was okay. Maybe those were the people who needed me and my testimony most of all. Truthfully, the bottom line came down to this: God wanted me at His Church, so no matter what, that's where I was going to be. He had a plan, and I trusted Him. I ended my prayer, took a deep breath, and walked inside the building.

I walked into church with an open, loving, and accepting heart and ended up receiving from others exactly what I gave out. My ward family immediately embraced me with love. Friendly faces introduced themselves to me and reached out in sweet friendship from the very first Sunday I attended. I'll never forget my first Relief Society class, where an arm was thrown around me and a friendly introduction was given only moments after I sat down. While I was nervous and feeling incredibly shy, the Spirit was strong. I knew with concrete certainty that I was in the exact place that God wanted me to be. It didn't take long for me to understand and appreciate that the special people of the McCall Second Ward had been hand-chosen by the Lord to take me under their wing, give me a safe place to grow in the gospel, and show me what unconditional love is. They taught me by example what ministering is truly meant to be.

Through much prayer and quiet time with God, I felt a loving, yet firm, push toward the commitment to begin attending a twelve-step recovery group. Even though I knew it meant directly facing my fear of being around strangers, I was being truly inspired to embrace this new fellowship. Terrified of being vulnerable, I again asked Heavenly Father to help me overcome my anxiety enough to walk through the front door. He supported my efforts by giving me that strength, and it wasn't long before I began attending meetings on a regular basis. The Spirit was unmistakable as people bravely shared their experience, strength, and hope with each other. There was something deeply refreshing about being in a room filled with people who knew exactly what it was like to live in a broken addict mind just like mine. From their mouths came my very thoughts, feelings, and experiences. They too knew of the powerlessness, had wandered for years in the hopelessness, and had lived many of the same horrors I had lived. They spoke of faith, surrender, and the magical power behind service. They were authentically happy and carried with them a contagious joy about God and life. Each was fixed in a firm hope of the future that they acknowledged was a direct result of their bold confidence in their Higher Power. The first thing I was taught was that there is no cure for the disease of addiction. While I am alive, the cunning, baffling, and powerful beast will never be slain and put to rest once and for all. What I can have, though, is a daily reprieve from my disease based solely on the maintenance of my spiritual condition. That means my recovery, which is rooted in my faith, must always be my number one priority. My recovery must come first so that everything and everyone I love in my life doesn't have to come last.

It seemed to me in this new life that every time I turned around I was being blessed by the Lord's elite. There was my mother's ninety-nine-year-old neighbor, Ursula, who, soon after I moved to McCall, asked me to be her caregiver. Her spunky personality and irreverent humor pulled me right out of my shell. Our special connection was obvious as we immediately bonded. While I served her strong cappuccinos just the way she liked them, I listened intently as she told me her stories of prohibition, War of the Worlds, and getting lost while hunting for morel mushrooms. While she was helping me transition from my old life into my new one, in turn, I was privileged to be able to help her do the same. I only had the chance to know Ursula for just 1 percent of her long, amazing life, but the impact her level of love and loyalty had on me was profound. I will always consider her one of my greatest friends. Because of the incredible joyful experience I had while working with Ursula, after she was gone I continued spending a portion of my time caregiving and made other close connections as a result.

Then there was Clyde and Marty Dillon. I met them in their role as a stake missionary couple. From the beginning, they treated me as though I was one of their own children. They helped support my recovery, believed in me in the moments I couldn't believe in myself, and were there for me with their time and anything else I needed. They made me feel comfortable enough to openly discuss my questions about scriptures or talk about some of the difficult spiritual experiences I'd had without fear of any judgment. I have learned much from their beautiful model of Christlike behavior. The standard they set is the one that I will use and reflect on as I go forth and try to serve others as they have served me.

My empty wasteland of an isolated life was blooming into a luscious garden with bright colors of friends, family connections, and bounties of love. It was as if the Lord had preordained and blessed me with an army of angels to be there during the unique moment of time in my life when I was stepping out of the darkness and into the light.

Reflecting back, it had become clear to me how hard The Whisperer had worked to throw up barriers between me and other people. When I was a young child he began trying to isolate me by convincing me that I was somehow broken and had been born with absolutely no value. He bombarded my mind and thoughts with mountains of shame and whispered lies into my ears that I wasn't worthy of love. How many years had I wasted believing his deceitful lies and in turn alienated myself from those who could have been great friends? How long had those negative thoughts and inaccurate beliefs driven a dividing wedge between me and the very people and places my soul craved and desired?

The Whisperer did not relent or immediately withdraw his noise campaign just because I was sober and turning to God for support. For a time he worked harder than ever to keep me walled off from others. He knew that for a while I would still drag a duffle bag stuffed with trauma and distrust around with me. Living life as a prostitute and then being trapped amongst the evil and depraved had altered the way I viewed others. I had learned that real monsters weren't obvious with claws and sharp pointy teeth. Real monsters looked like businessmen, plumbers, or dads playing with their kids at the park. They drove minivans, had library cards, and were registered voters. Going about my daily business, it was easy for my mind to wonder about the man at the gas station who politely stopped to open the door for me. What evil thoughts could he be hiding behind his phony cordial smile?

As The Whisperer flooded my mind with those wild and skeptical thoughts, it became clear to me that I had an important choice to make in moving forward. I was either going to continue to be afraid and see people for the worst they could be, or I was going to flip the script and choose to see everyone around me only as loved children of God. It is true that there are those in this world who choose to participate in secret works of darkness, with motives and moving components that are difficult and even maddening to grasp and understand. But all I ever got by putting my focus on that unfortunate truth was a heavy push right back down the rabbit hole. To be honest, I'd had enough of Wonderland for one lifetime. So with conviction, I pushed my chair out from the Mad Hatter's table, and choosing to leave all his vain riddles unsolved, I turned my back on Wonderland forever. I put all of my focus on God's love instead.

23.
A Brand-New World

From the time I was a small child, once I had lived through any damaging experience, the pain of it never left me. Like a permanent stain, I absorbed and then trapped the suffering forever within the walls of my soul. As I walked down the path of my life, I collected troubles, sorrows, and the burdens of my sins like some people collect rocks or seashells. At first the pebbles were small enough that I could keep them hidden away from the world in the bottom of my pockets, and for a season, I hardly even noticed they were there. But over time, the injuries grew in size and the weight of the load became more and more difficult to bear. The pebbles became rocks and the rocks became boulders. Then they stacked high and heavy and filled my arms. Like a perverse magic trick, the rubble multiplied and the jagged pressure began to lacerate my skin and fracture my bones.

As I trudged my way under the immense weight and pain, one frantic and furious thought raced through my mind: *What cold-blooded monster is the Great Designer behind this madness?*

While I chewed on that bitter speculation, fear cast a long shadow of impending doom. In my heart of hearts, I always knew that I wasn't going to be able to carry my rocks forever. I waited in terror for the awful day when I would finally buckle and collapse under the weight.

My dark premonition had been right all along, and with eerie exactness, the catastrophe came at the most inopportune moment in time. I was trapped in a den of devils the day I heard the groaning of the earth and felt the rumble of the landslide. Frozen in place, I watched the enormous mass of debris sliding toward me. There wasn't any time for me to run, and there certainly wasn't anywhere left for me to go. When the dust finally settled, I was pinned helpless beneath a mountain of rubble. Completely conquered and wholly defeated, every particle of my toxic pride had been crushed in the devastation. With the obliteration of my ego, my degrading humiliation transformed into heavenly humility. My spirit finally relented its choke hold of control, and I unconditionally surrendered. With my final breath, I cried out.

"Oh God, have mercy on me."

If one had been looking through spiritual eyes only, then I would have been quite a sorry sight to see the day I limped into my bishop's office. Like I had just come home from war, all that could be seen were the dark bruises, the bloody makeshift bandages holding me together, and the look of defeat in my tired eyes. With battered and broken arms, I began holding up my rocks one by one for my bishop to examine up close and personal. Taking absolutely nothing with me to the grave, I confessed it all. Then pointing at my heap of shame and sorrows, I told him I didn't want it anymore, and I swore that I couldn't take another step forward with it.

With the bit in my mouth and the yoke on my back, I declared to him firmly, "I forsake. I forsake. I forsake."

I spent my entire life feeling abandoned by a callous God. I wondered why it all had to be so painful. Why did I have to be tortured by a shaming voice in my head and have emotions that cut me like a knife? Why couldn't I just be normal like everyone else? Why did my dad have to die and leave me when I was so young? Why did a confusing disease called addiction have to ravage my mind, body, and soul, turning me into a shell of a human? Why did earth life have to be so incredibly hard? Most of all, why would a loving God do this to His child?

Over the years, those were the difficult questions that circled round and round on a track through my head. It wasn't until I turned to the Savior in bold faith and complete trust that I began to understand the enigma behind all of the pain. It was only when I let go, closed my eyes, and did the trust fall back into His arms that the mystery of all of the suffering was solved. I understand now that Heavenly Father gave me my many weaknesses as a kind gift. The mental health issues and the terrible addictive tendencies were, in fact, endowed to me by perfect design.

Poisonous pride that camouflaged as insecurity, self-righteousness, and crowned victimhood blinded my eyes and became the deep gulf that separated me from God and His healing power. My weaknesses worked together to create the critical tipping point where the pain of the problem could finally become greater than the pain of the solution. It took the enormous emotional suffering brought on by my shortcomings for me to be compelled to reach the humility I needed in order to truly turn to God. Without the blessing of all of my God-given weaknesses, I would not, and could not know Him like I do today.

The name Jesus Christ has meant many different things to me over the vast span of my lifetime. When I was a little girl, I was taught about His birth and His life of ministry. It had been explained to me that Jesus was born into the world as the sacrificial lamb by a virgin mother named Mary. I had sung songs in Primary about my desire to be like Him and to go home and live with Him one day. "He loves you, and He gave His life for you," I was told, and for the tiniest sliver of time, I lived in that truth. But then the savage whirlwinds came and scraped away everything I loved, including my father, and I placed all the blame of the pain on Christ. Like acid, the bitterness corroded away the delicate testimony I had once had, and in the great distance I put between us, I had reduced Jesus Christ to a joke. As I turned Him into a bad punch line, I'd have sworn up and down I didn't care one way another about the subject, and for a time, I didn't. My denial of His reality became the concrete shell around my heart, and underneath all the anguish and suffering, I swore at Him. In my boiling rage at the meager condition of my life, I mocked Him, and had He been standing in front of me, I would have spit on Him. With a long nail in one hand and holding firm to the hammer in the other, I loudly declared that He was guilty, and then I convicted and sentenced Him to death. Despite all of my years of cruelty and misplaced rage, when I finally ran to Him and begged for His forgiveness, He was there with open arms to receive me.

Jesus Christ was never the monster I had constructed out of broken ideas. Nor was He the barbarian I created Him to be in order to take my rightful place as victim. It was my lack of understanding of who He was that kept me chained to The Beast for nearly a lifetime. As I have begun to really know the Savior, I have found out that He is not the villain of my story. Instead, He is the Hero. He is my soul protector, my spirit deliverer, and my light in the dark and twisting wilderness.

It wasn't until I started handing over my rocks to Jesus Christ, with complete faith in Him, that I began to see the exciting miracles that are born of His great sacrifice. Christ's Atonement isn't some mystical power that, like a mirage, floats just outside of my grasp. It isn't a fantasy, a really nice idea, or an abstract concept too foreign for me to access. The Atonement of Jesus Christ is right here, right now, and powerful enough to alter the very reality that I exist in.

I had always mistakenly believed that because of all the terrible things I had done, that in order for me to ever feel worthy again, my rocks would have to taken far away and buried down a deep hole somewhere. With the layers of scarlet letters on my arm, the only way I could ever imagine being able to hold my head up high in this world would be if my sins were completely erased from my mind, not to mention everyone else's. It is my witness that the transformative power behind the Atonement of Jesus Christ is much more magnificent than that sad prospect. Instead of deleting my past, the Savior's Atonement literally takes my weaknesses and transforms them into my strengths. In other words, He takes my rocks of suffering and boulders of sins and builds me a brand-new world out of them.

It has been shown that no one can reach and help an addict like another addict. Without the amazing recovering addicts who were willing to share their years of experience, strength, and hope with me, I would have been unable to see the possibility of recovery for my life. An addict in recovery is uniquely qualified to reach someone suffering from addiction and can help where no one else can. Only because of my grueling life experience in the disease are other addicts able to see themselves in my story. Once they relate, they can grasp onto and believe in the hope for themselves. The Savior took my rocks and He built pathways to others who are suffering as I once suffered. He constructed bridges for me to cross over to reach those who are isolated and alone in the fear and the despair of addiction. He built me a tower high above the earth, and from my new heavenly perspective, I see the greater purpose of my life. The Savior shares His light with me, and because He does, I can join in the joyful work alongside the other lantern holders. In unity, we carry the message of recovery and hope to others, and all of that is only possible because of Him.

I have been asked before if I would take any of it back if I could. If I had the option, would I delete all those years of suffering and pain? Would I change my difficult life of addiction and choose an easier journey instead? The truth is this: I would go through it all again to know what I know today. I would live through every second of the agony and experiences, every moment of the suffering, if that's what it took to gain the testimony of Jesus Christ that I have today. Every single second of it.

Today, I still have questions, but they are different than they once were, and I ask them with a grateful heart already knowing the answers. How would I have ever known the sweet if I hadn't had to choke down a large dose of the bitter? How could I ever have understood the Savior's powerful grace without the opportunity to be healed by Him? How would I have ever really known His tremendous goodness and capacity to love without the chance to experience that His loving mercy was the only thing that could save me? I see and accept that it was, in fact, the only way.

On April 28, 2018, my forty-third birthday, I went through the Meridian Idaho Temple to receive my endowment and to make my covenants with the Lord. Many came that day to witness the miracle with their own eyes. Kari, Heather, and Garin were there, as well as many other friends, including, of course, Clyde and Marty Dillon. When Patrick and his wife found out I was going through the temple, they drove all the way from the Midwest to be there and show their support. Afterward, we all gathered in front of the beautiful temple to talk and take pictures. Those around us stood quietly in reverence as Kari, Heather, and I stood in a circle, crying tears of joy and holding each other.

How grateful I am to the Lord for opening the veil that day in a dingy motel bathroom and for giving my dad the opportunity to share the spark of hope that I so desperately needed. It was the light from that spark that I hung onto as I finished the final leg of my dark and difficult journey. It is that spark I have since kindled and carefully nursed into the raging fire that burns bright in my soul today.

"You are going to write something that is going to make a difference in people's lives. Your experience is going to help others," he told me.

My dad was right. I do have an important message to share with you.

Difficult mental illness has been my constant companion since I was a little girl. I am covered in the scars I gave to myself trying to quiet the monsters in my head. I have cursed God, sold my soul to the devil, and abandoned my children for drugs. I am a gutter-level junkie who supported her drug habit in the filthy underworld of prostitution. I lived for years alone in a motel room with a mind full of demons and a needle full of drugs. I have worn shameful labels and bore humiliating names like crazy, weak, and worst of all, worthless. I have lain alone in a cold, dark box, buried alive by my addictions, and listened to the heart-broken whispers from six feet above my head.

"There is nothing we can do to help her. It's time to let her go."

Through the world's eyes, my situation was hopeless. After a lifetime of circling the drain, recovery was more than unlikely. Some even said it was impossible. Addiction was my Goliath, the mighty giant in front of me, and having used up all of my strength, I had been defeated by it. But I have learned from my gospel studies and my own experience that the Lord often employs the underdog to show His strength. The more impossible the circumstance, the more obvious His miracles become. I am eternally grateful to Jesus Christ for His mercy, and I am proud to stand as a witness of the reality of His grace.

Because of the Savior, there is hope for me today. Because of the Savior, there is hope for everyone.

There is hope.
There is hope.
There is hope.

To my earthly father: I love you. I made it just like you said I would. I made it all the way home.

Kelly Thompson

Kelly Thompson is a recovering heroin/meth addict and alcoholic who spent twenty-eight years battling the disease of addiction. Plagued by mental illness and drug use, she hit rock bottom, which included homelessness and prostitution. Through the Atonement of Jesus Christ and 12-Step Recovery, her life transformed from one of tragedy and despair into one of purpose, light, and joy. Once a self-proclaimed atheist, she is now an active member of The Church of Jesus Christ of Latter-day Saints.

As a child, Kelly had a passion for writing and was encouraged by her father to pursue it. Twenty-five years later, she was instead a homeless prostitute trapped in the dark underworld of the streets of Salt Lake City. Near death and in the throes of heroin and meth addiction, she experienced a heavenly visit that changed everything. She's been writing about the hope of addiction recovery through the Atonement of Jesus Christ ever since. Her many years of personal struggle with mental illness and drug addiction have enabled her to write about and give unique insight into the mysterious inner workings of an addict's mind.

Kelly is an author, a public speaker, and a social media influencer who is dedicated to sharing the real hope available with those who continue to suffer.

Scan to visit

kellythompsonauthor.com